Dance in the End Zone

The Business Owner's Exit
Planning Playbook

Published by Camarillo Press
Atlanta, Georgia 30327

Dance in the End Zone
ISBN: 978-1-935038-21-4

Cover design by Max2o.

Printed in the United States of America.

To Mom and Dad for filling my mind, Larry for challenging my goals and most importantly to Stephanie for sharing my journey.

Disclaimer

The book discusses various tax, legal and financial tools, tactics and regulations that may assist you with developing and implementing a successful exit plan. While the author has made the best effort to carefully and accurately present these tools, tactics and regulations, the reader must take into account his specific situation and consult with his advisors before reaching any conclusions or taking action. This information is not intended for, nor can it be used by any taxpayer for the purpose of avoiding federal taxes or penalties. Furthermore, there are a number of important issues that because of space this book cannot address such as tax and legal considerations in your state. The guidance offered in this book in some cases may not be appropriate for your situation.

The reader would grow tedious if every topic or point ended with, "Please consult your tax, legal and financial advisors on your specific situation." However, that is exactly what is required.

Acknowledgements

This book would never have happened without help from many people. Some know of their contribution and some do not. I would like to thank the business owners whom I have had the pleasure to know and work with in their exit planning. As a group they are caring, dedicated, passionate leaders who do not get the recognition they deserve from society. It has been a pleasure to serve them.

My partners and colleagues at White Horse Advisors all contributed to this book. Their professionalism, hard work and humor create a special firm. Several deserve special note: Jeff Weronick for being a "jam-up" compliance officer, Stephanie Bova for her edits and pasta, and Dennis Melde and my father Tom for support only partners can provide.

I owe a debt to the entire Vistage International community. More than five hundred Vistage members and chairs participated in the research that made this book possible. I do not know most of their names but appreciate their time and assistance. Several Vistage individuals I can and must acknowledge by name: Jansen Chazanof for his guiding spirit, Lisa Dugan for her enthusiasm and Larry Hart for asking all the tough questions. My cohorts in Vistage 603 stood at the heart of this effort—my desire to meet their standards drove the book's completion. A special thank you to the following 603ers: Michael Wilkinson for advice and checking-in along the way, Ann Herrmann-Nehdi for her ideas and excitement, and David Taylor-Klaus for the humor and sounding board.

Several organizations have my thanks for their expertise and willingness to go the extra steps: Chet Zalesky and the research team at CMI, Kimberly Boim at the World Wide Association of Writers, and Tom, Rob and Shelly from Max2o. Erica Stephens and the team from Weaver-Stephens also have my gratitude. Erica and "the ladies" gave the name on the cover and so much more.

I am most grateful to my family for their care and support each step along the way. My wife Stephanie stands above all others as my editor, consultant, cheerleader, researcher, guide and friend.

Author's Notes

For simplicity this book assumes that each business owner owns only one business. Of course one individual may own multiple businesses, just as one business may have multiple owners. The text will specify multiple businesses or multiple owners where relevant.

Closely-held businesses take many legal forms including corporations, partnerships, limited liability companies (LLCs) and others. Owners of corporations are *shareholders*, owners of partnerships are *partners* and owners of LLCs are *members*. Unless necessary to differentiate between one legal form and another, I use the general term *owner* to include all of the above.

Throughout the book you will encounter short "Real World Stories" that share experiences of actual business owners, usually clients past and present. Most readers find stories helpful for understanding complex issues and relating the material to their situation. Please keep in mind that circumstances differ from business owner to business owner and the experiences of those in the Real World Stories may not the same as your experiences, even in seemingly similar situations. In all cases, names and other identifying details have been changed to protect privacy.

Many real world stories and other issues addressed in the book require numbers to make the point. Generally I have used simple numbers that are relevant to the context to avoid the math from getting in the way. For example, a story may state the closely-held business was worth $10 million. In most cases you may add or subtract zeros to make the numbers relevant to your situation.

For convenience and clarity, I have used the male pronouns "him" and "he" when referring to business owners and other persons. I applaud the increasing number of women-owned businesses, and look forward to the time when people more skilled than me in the grammatical arts figure out a way to reference both genders yet still write in a readable manner.

Table of Contents

1

The End Zone

On November 18, 1973 Elmo Wright, a wide receiver for the Kansas City Chiefs professional football team, scored a touchdown in a game against the Houston Oilers. As far as touchdowns go, it was not remarkable. What happened after was. Elmo Wright danced in the end zone. He is believed to be the first player to celebrate a touchdown in such a memorable and distinct manner. You don't have to be a sports fan to appreciate the emotions that a really good end zone dance conveys: celebration, accomplishment, success. It's contagious, affecting teammates and fans alike. In an interview with the *New York Times* more than thirty years later, Elmo Wright said, "I've accomplished a lot in my life, but what happened in the end zone is what defines my career."

If you are the owner of a closely-held business, you have something in common with Elmo. Most owners invest decades of sweat, risk and sacrifice into their businesses. Business success may already have brought you personal sense of achievement and significant financial rewards. Yet what happens when you exit your business, when you reach your end zone, likely defines your career too. An exit that falls short can mean financial disappointment, family strife or loss of self-esteem. I have witnessed many owners face this after years or decades of business success. Your exit should be the crowning achievement of a career, the fulfillment of financial and family dreams, the next chapter in a business legacy. It is a cause for celebrating—for dancing in the end zone like Elmo once did. After all, you've likely worked too hard to not do what is necessary to be successful in the end. The sole purpose of this book is to offer practical, understandable and applicable help to closely-held business owners who want to dance in the end zone.

There is an important item to address up front. What if you are unsure or do not believe that you would ever want to exit? Many successful owners feel this way. They love what they do, enjoy the business challenges and want to work as long as health and life allow. If you feel this way, congratulations for getting this far into a book on exit planning (perhaps somebody pressured you to read this) and hang in there a bit longer. In my nearly twenty years experience working with business owners, those who "never want to exit" have been given a poor explanation of what exit planning means for them. If you enjoy owning and working in your business that much, you probably care deeply about it. We do not live forever, so exit planning is partially about making real your vision of a business legacy.

Additionally, most owners who do not want to stop working still aspire to achieve "financial freedom" which is the ability to enjoy your desired lifestyle without earned income. In other words, you work because you chose not because you must. As we will explore in this book, our approach to exit planning emphasizes using the business to achieve financial freedom whether you stop working on that exact day or not. Finally there is also a risk management aspect; if you want to work as long as possible then you should take reasonable steps to prevent anything from derailing your ability to do so. Putting exit planning into this light may change your understanding of what this is about.

Too many owners are ill prepared for their inevitable exit. In my career, I constantly encounter successful owners who have paid little attention to this critical topic. As a result, as exit draws near they find themselves scrambling to gain control over the situation, needing to radically change their businesses and losing significant value to high taxes and other costs. To explore this further, my firm, White Horse Advisors, recently conducted a national survey on exit planning and closely-held business owners. An independent market research firm surveyed nearly 450 owners, asking dozens of questions exploring exit goals, concerns and level of preparation. Findings from the research will be shared throughout this book. However, one finding stands above all others: owners know planning for their exit is important but few, if any, have conducted any serious planning. In the research, nearly nine of ten owners stated that an exit plan was important to their future and their business futures, but less than one out of ten had a current, written exit plan.[*]

In Table 1-1, owners were asked to indicate how well they had addressed the key concepts of exit planning. In nearly all areas the strong majority of owners shared they had not completely addressed the topic. In perhaps the most concerning area, 95% of owners' advisory teams are not meeting with each other and working from a written game plan. Elmo Wright could not have scored many touchdowns if his team never met together or did not use a Playbook. We will explore later in the book who needs to be on your exit planning team and how that team functions. Throughout this book we also will share stories of real owners whose lack of preparation made their exit more expensive and painful than necessary, or who lost altogether the opportunity to dance in the end zone.

Table 1-1: Areas of Owner Preparedness for Exit

Statement	Owners who answered "Yes, I have completely addressed this."
I own adequate disability and life insurance should I become disabled or prematurely die.	61%
I have a team of advisors who are qualified to meet my entire exit planning needs.	29%
I have identified in writing the net value I need from the business to afford retirement or my other post exit financial goals.	27%
I have identified and implemented tactics to mitigate creditor risk against my business and personal assets.	21%
I have put in place formal, written compensation programs to retain my top employees and reduce the risk that their loss would undermine my exit plans.	20%
I have fully shared with my loved ones my exit plans, goals and strategy and have their support.	20%
I have a clear vision of what I want to do and accomplish in life after my exit.	12%

[*] White Horse Advisors 2008 Survey of Closely-held Business Owners. See the Appendix for more information about the research.

I have a written analysis of my exit strategy's tax impact and have implemented the tactics available to minimize these taxes.	9%
My team of advisors meets as a group, has a clearly defined leader and works from a written exit plan.	5%

Source: White Horse Advisors 2008 Survey of Closely-Held Business Owners

Why are Owners So Unprepared?

The lack of adequate preparation is not difficult to diagnose, but is important to understand. First, most owners are just plain busy. With daily business demands it's easy to ignore an issue that you believe is ten, twenty or thirty years down the road. As a client once said, "When I'm so busy keeping it going, I can't be thinking about the finish."

Another reason owners are ill-prepared is planning for exit is not easy. For most owners, the business is the primary if not sole source of income and wealth. The business holds your wealth hostage. Most closely-held businesses are illiquid, difficult to value and vulnerable to an immense range of risks—only some of which owners can influence or control. Exiting and freeing the captive wealth can be complex and costly, especially in terms of taxes. To make matters worse, owners struggle to find good help. While a nearly endless supply of consultants, academic programs, books and workshops teach how to start and grow a business, few help with how to exit. In the same research study cited above, about one in six owners stated that the primary reason they have not addressed this issue is they did not know where to get help.

The third reason owners are unprepared, and probably the most harmful misconception about exit planning, is owners believe this issue can safely wait until just a few years prior to your desired exit. Nobody faults you for believing (up to now) that this issue can wait. The marketplace seems to be telling you it's alright to wait every time you receive one of those unsolicited phone calls or emails asking if your business is for sale. All that activity suggests that soon as you are ready to exit, a buyer will be waiting in the wings. In addition to the market suggesting it's safe to wait, your own advisors or peers may have told that exit planning can wait until three to five years before you are "ready" to exit.

The Five Years Fallacy

Much of the conventional wisdom suggests you should start serious planning about five years before you are ready to exit. This misperception is so common we call it the Five Years Fallacy. There are four major flaws with this approach. First, there are many tactics that can take longer than five years to implement. If you restrict yourself to five years or less, you risk forfeiting using these tools or reducing their effectiveness. Consider the following ways five years may often be insufficient time to achieve the maximum success:

- Selecting the ideal business entity is an important consideration, especially in the event of a sale, because the type of business entity may greatly impact taxes. For example, owners of C corporations in some cases may reduce taxes upon a sale by converting to S corporation status prior to sale. However, the tax benefits can be lost if the company is subsequently sold within a ten year holding period after conversion. In another example the reverse may be true— owners of S corporations seeking to implement an ESOP as an exit strategy may secure tax free proceeds from the sale if they convert to a regular C corporation. Matching up your exit plan with the appropriate business entity may require years to implement. It is best to consult with a business attorney.

- Owners seeking to pass a business down to the next family generation often desire to make tax free gifts of business interests to the successor generation. Congress limits the value of gifts that can be made without triggering gift or estate taxes, including annual gift limits. As a result passing down a large family business can take many years to accomplish. Too little time inhibits the effectiveness of gifts and other family-business transfer strategies.

- If you intend to sell to a third party buyer, your business' intellectual property may be an important factor in driving value at sale. US law sets timelines required to register, file and protect your intellectual property. If you wait until five years or less to develop an intellectual property strategy, likely you will have forfeited many of the rights and opportunities available to grow value.

- Owners seeking to sell their business to one or more employees need to hire, train and groom a key employee or entire team prepared to run your business. Developing successor leadership may take many years.

- Many exit tactics benefit from the "miracle of compound growth" on invested assets. For example, funding an income tax deductible retirement plan creates potential future income outside the business. If you have only a few years to implement this tactic, your results likely will be greatly diminished.

The second major flaw with limiting your preparation time to five years (or less) is if you intend to sell the business, you cannot control many factors that impact the business's price. Broad market conditions, interest rates, capital markets, your industry's health and other external forces influence the availability of cash, the cost of capital and the demand for businesses in your industry or market. Many economists note that these cycles can take as long as seven to ten years to cycle. If you are restricted to exiting within a specific time frame such as five years, you may choose a time when your business's price is lower due to external conditions. Your financial advisor probably has been telling you "Don't try to time the market," when investing in publicly traded stocks, bonds and mutual funds. But when it comes to selling your business, you must try to time the market. Leaving only a few years' preparation to sell may limit the ability to achieve the most favorable external climate.

Market Timing Mistake

Robert was the sole owner of a successful business with two key employees who wanted to buy him out at some point. One day Robert told his two employees he wanted to be bought out in two years. Robert had become increasingly tired of the business and was eager to pursue a lifelong dream of teaching at a local business college. The two employees and Robert began to map out their transition plans.

While this was underway, interest rates rose and this business's industry grew soft. The employees could see their costs of borrowing money to buy out Robert increasing right at a time the business margins were shrinking. The business was sold two years later, but the employees were unable to put as much cash down as Robert had hoped. The employees came to resent Robert after years of good relations because they had to take over in the middle of a difficult business environment. Robert disliked how much owner financing he had to provide because the employees could not raise as much cash. More time

> might have permitted a happier new beginning for the two key
> employees and a happier ending for Robert.

The third major flaw with limiting your exit planning preparations to the last five years is simply you cannot predict the future. A prospective buyer with a large checkbook may walk through your front door tomorrow. Your industry may go through an unexpected consolidation (often called a "rollup") which heats up your potential market price, but only for a window of time. You may become seriously disabled and unable to work. You may die. Who guarantees how much time you have? Life happens.

The fourth and final reason why you cannot wait to start serious exit planning is that if you have not clearly defined where you want to end up, then you do not know if the decisions you are making today will get you there. In Stephen Covey's best-selling book *Seven Habits of Highly Effective People*, the second habit is to "Begin with the End in Mind." His lesson applies here. To paraphrase Mr. Covey, the successful owner must be able to visualize the desired outcome and concentrate on activities which help achieve success in the end zone. Align your *business growth plan* with your *business exit plan*. Making today's important business decisions without considering the ultimate impact on your exit potentially causes great difficulties down the road.

The $7 Million Oops

Jim owned a business that his father had founded nearly thirty years earlier. Jim wanted his only daughter to one day make the business a third-generation company. About five years before we met Jim, he had established a second company because their business was expanding into a horizontal market. Jim's advisors recommended at that time that the new company be created with fifty-fifty ownership between father and daughter to reflect their joint management role. Jim and his daughter grew the new company into a $35 million business in just five years time.

When we met Jim, he asked us to make sure his daughter inherited the businesses at minimal costs. Setting up the new company fifty-fifty between Jim and his daughter may have been an understandable management decision, but it was a poor exit decision. When Jim eventually passes his half of the second business to his daughter, he faced about $7 million in out of pocket transfer taxes. A smarter exit decision would have been to put most of the new company in the daughter's name when its value was practically nothing. This likely would have avoided a $7 million potential tax bill. (Jim could still maintain managerial control of the business by keeping for himself most or all of the company's voting stock and limiting his daughter's interest at this time to non-voting stock.) Beginning with the end in mind aligns current business needs with the future exit plans.

In our work, we are often undoing or working around decisions that the owner made years earlier—decisions that may have been different if the owner or his advisors had considered the future exit. Whether you want to exit within the next five years or feel you have more time, you must start serious exit planning now. Planning now reduces risk that the decisions made today will create problems at exit.

A Better Way (Exit Planning is Not What You Think)

The conventional approach to exit planning not only starts too late, but also aims at the wrong needs. Too often your needs from and for the business are downplayed and ignored. Evidence may be found in how "exit planning" is often confused with "succession planning." The terms are not synonymous. Wall Street, the realm of publicly traded companies, does not discuss *exit planning* yet frequently examines the *succession planning* issues. When publicly traded company executives or analysts discuss succession planning they are referring to the orderly transfer of business leadership from one team to the next. Publicly traded company leaders have little need to discuss exit planning. Exiting for the shareholder in a publicly traded company can be as simple as telling the stock broker to sell the shares, often accomplished by the end of that day's trading. The difference is important. If a term does not have a clearly understood meaning then it's likely to find confusion and errors. Imagine if surgeons routinely confused "lobotomy" with "tracheotomy." People would end up with holes in the wrong place in their heads.

If succession planning focuses on meeting the needs of the *business*, then exit planning aims to meet the needs of the *owner*. Mixing up the two phrases blurs how to achieve your objectives. A sound succession plan does not automatically produce a successful exit, and vice versa. Succession planning's measurement of success is the business's continuation; if the business survived the management succession then the plan worked. While you may be deeply committed to your businesses' long term survival, your personal and financial goals should not be ignored but rather of primary importance. Remember, an exit that achieves orderly succession but leaves you financially vulnerable or without peace of mind is not a successful exit.

To achieve better results we need to start with a clear understanding of what exit planning should be about, when to get started, and how it benefits you both today and in the future. In the research for this book, we could not find a definition of *exit planning* that addresses common owner goals outside orderly management succession. The lack of clarity undermines owners' appreciation for the need to begin with the end in mind and the benefits created in the process. A client once made this clearer than I ever had. Shortly into our work for him, he interrupted a point I was making and exclaimed, "You know, exit planning is not what I thought it was!" To get us off to a strong start, this book offers, to the best of my knowledge, the first formal *exit planning* definition that addresses your goals and objectives:

> **Exit planning is the conscious effort to grow your business in a manner that efficiently converts ownership into personal financial freedom and peace of mind.**

Breaking down the definition's components helps explain the value:

- *"...conscious effort..."* – Exit planning requires that you, with assistance from experienced advisors, take specific steps to achieve superior results and avoid undesirable outcomes. Rarely will putting your head down, ignoring the future and risks along the way produce the best results. Doing nothing risks forfeiting control. As you grow your business, the decisions you make should take into account and support the ultimate exit goals.

- *"...to grow your business in a manner that..."* – Imagine two businesses from the same industry with similar locations, revenues and profits are in a room together. Given the similarities, the two businesses will be worth about the same value—right? And the two owners could each expect about the same results at exit—right? Not necessarily. Depending on how those businesses were grown, one business may be worth far more than the other and one owner may face a far easier and more successful exit than the other. A superior definition for exit planning includes aligning what is best for *growing* the business with what is best for *exiting* the business. Otherwise, you risk arriving at your ideal exit time only to find the picture more difficult, more expensive and more heavily taxed than things could have been.

- *"...efficiently converts ownership..."* – Exiting from a business can be expensive, especially in terms of taxes. Depending on the situation, federal income taxes alone may reach 69% or more of the assessed value of the business combined between the buyer and seller. State income or sales taxes may add to this total. Estate taxes may pose an additional threat. A sound exit plan must reduce taxes and other costs where possible to maximize net results.

- *"...into personal financial freedom and peace of mind."* – An exit that leaves you unable to afford your post exit financial goals, or in some way feeling regretful, is likely a failed exit. In our research and my experience, most owners' number one goal at exit is to achieve "financial freedom." This does not mean retirement; you may continue to work and earn a paycheck for a long time. Financial freedom means that you do not *need* a paycheck; you can afford your desired lifestyle without any earned income. (If you are still working in some capacity, your income is gravy.) Financial freedom is the whole story for most owners, however. A successful exit also must leave you with peace of mind that you did it the right way. In my experience owners define peace of mind in many different ways, but it's usually a mix of what was right for the business, for your family and for yourself. This last component of the exit planning definition says that at some point the business should serve your needs and not always the other way around.

Exit Planning Creates a Better Business Today

Up to this point we've discussed and demonstrated the need to start serious exit planning now in order to create the best opportunity to dance in the end zone. However, some good news—you do not have to wait that long to see the benefits of your exit planning. Effective exit planning can create a better business today. A better business may provide you with more options in your exit planning, more flexibility and more fun. That's a lot to suggest is possible, so let's see how.

Sound exit planning requires a hard assessment of what your business needs to look like to fulfill your exit goals, and what is needed to get it there. When building a business with the end in mind, it's not enough to just grow revenues or make more money each year. *How you get there becomes as important as the results* because exit planning holds your business up to a brighter light. It forces you to consider not only what you and the business need today, but also what is needed in the future. Taking action to meet those needs creates a potentially better business today.

Let's do a couple examples of how planning for your future exit can create a better business today. Assume that we are speaking with an owner who wants to sell his business for the maximum value to a third party. Imagine it's the future and this owner is actually meeting with a potential buyer. He is pleased to announce that revenues are up 25% over prior year. The buyer is likely to say "Great, how did you do this?" The owner's answer will impact how much the buyer is willing to pay for the business. Assume the answer is something along these lines:

> "Well, most the clients know me and have worked with me for a long time. Over the last few years I have really focused on sales so revenues are up."

Hearing this answer, that buyer is probably reducing in his head the price he is willing to pay. Contrast the first hypothetical answer with this second:

> "Well, our business development team—headed up by our bright young VP of Sales—has really established a competitive edge in core markets. Several years of effort are just starting to take off."

This second answer is probably increasing the business's price with every passing minute. In both answers, sales were up 25%. Yet how the revenue increases were accomplished quite differently. In the first answer, results were tied to the owner's efforts. If that owner exited the business, or just got tired of going on sales calls, it appears much of that revenue could be lost. The second answer unquestionably reveals a better business. The business will grow without its owner going on individual sales calls and has established competitive advantages that likely create numerous positives within the business.

Consider another example. Assume for a moment we are speaking with an owner who desires to sell the business to one or more top employees. Most business owners recognize the need to motivate and retain top talent. However, if an owner intends to sell his business to his employees, motivating and retaining them becomes far more important. Let's give two hypothetical explanations for how this owner might approach this issue. The first is:

> "My top people are truly loyal to me. They trust that I will take care of them and treat them fairly. As for motivating them, I pay cash bonuses based on how well I feel everybody did."

Contrast the first hypothetical answer with this approach:

> "While I have great relationships with my top employees, we feel that is not enough in today's competitive marketplace. Several years ago we developed a phantom stock program that ties their rewards to key business results. If the employees quit, they forfeit the phantom stock. If they stay and buy my business, the phantom stock is convertible to cash to help fund the purchase from me."

Both approaches could work. But in the first approach, motivation and retention is based on personal loyalty. How cohesive and effective with that management team be once the current owner is gone? The second approach clearly creates a better business today. That business has less risk of key employees leaving early and compensation is tied to measurable performance. Under the second approach the owner also has begun to address the difficult issue of how the employees are going to be able to afford his buyout.

This book shares tactics are presented to help reach your end zone dance, but most offer the potential to improve your business today. The reality is a business prepared for the owner's exit is a better business. When owners realize this, often they say something like, "If my business ran that well I would not want to leave it." My answer is exactly! If you want to leave your business, then something may be wrong. That's not the ideal time or manner to exit. *The ideal business to exit is probably the one you most want to keep.* A better business today creates more options for you, more flexibility in your exit planning and is probably more fun.

Baby Boomer Business Owners

The need for owners to get ahead with their exit planning is growing. The aging Baby Boomer population may flood the market with owners seeking to exit over the next ten to fifteen years, making it difficult for owners who have fallen behind. Of the estimated 15 to 18 million American closely-held business owners,* the majority are Boomers. If the World War Two generation was America's greatest, then the Baby Boomer generation is America's *entrepreneurialist*. Never before in history have there been more closely-held businesses and owners than exists today. Their exits likely will impact every industry, market and community.

The Boomer phenomenon is significant for two reasons: 1) The huge increase in births starting in 1946 and 2) the deep decline in births after the Boomer wave ended in 1964. The combined effect is too many Boomers exiting with too few people to take over all these businesses. According to the Bureau of Labor Statistics, the percentage of workers age 24 to 34 is growing at about 8% while the group from age 35 to 44, immediately behind the Baby Boomers, is falling by 10% from 2000 to 2010. Ken Dychtwald, a noted speaker on Baby Boomer trends and author of the best selling *Age Wave*, addressed this shortage on the overall US labor population. He wrote, "We will have too few young workforce entrants to replace the labor, skills and talent of boomer retirees...Since the generation after the boomers is much smaller, companies can no longer rely upon a relative profusion of younger workers."[†] While Mr. Dychtwald is addressing the broad US labor market in his comments, the impact on business owners and their exit planning may be no less severe.

Fewer younger workers may hamper current owners' exit plans in a number of ways. The supply of businesses for sale may exceed the demand, lowering prices for businesses or at least making selling a business harder. Good successor management may be harder to come by, or hold on to if you have them. Economic or tax policies may change if the decline in the number

---

* The United States Census Bureau stated in 2004 there were about 5.5 million US businesses with at least one employee. Having at least one employee suggests an ongoing business exists beyond a holding company. In our experience the average privately held business has about three owners. Therefore 5.5 million times three is about 15 to 18 million business owners.

† *Workforce Crisis*, Ken Dychtwald. Harvard Business School Press, 2006.

of closely-held businesses is too great. The ultimate effects are unknown. The burden that these external forces may block a successful exit lies with current owners. We must devise and implement the most effective exit strategy possible to reduce the risk of this occurring in defense.

What Does an Exit Plan Look Like?

By now you may be convinced that you need an exit plan and should get started on it right away. If so, we need to discuss just what exactly is an exit plan? According to our research, nine of ten owners stated they do not have a current, written exit plan. Most owners need guidance on what a sound plan looks like. I am not an architect, but if I looked at a set of blueprints for a new home I could probably tell if critical things were missing like walls, electrical lines or plumbing. Unfortunately most owners have no idea what should go into an exit plan. The marketplace offers very little guidance too. Owners have shown me "exit plans" that range from as few as one page to book-length reports over a hundred pages long. Some have included detailed financial modeling and some have not. Some were co-written by a team of advisors, others created by just one person. Some were provided to the owner for no cost, while I have seen others that cost $100,000.

A thorough and sound exit plan needs to address six areas. If a plan fails to consider any one of these areas, it could not only miss an issue but possibly cause more harm than good.

1) Tax	The plan should create as much tax efficiency as is legally possible as we convert your business ownership into personal wealth.
2) Legal	The plan should use sound legal tactics and instruments to protect you and your business.
3) Financial	An exit plan accurately models and plans for how you achieve your post exit financial goals such as financial freedom.
4) Operational	The exit plan should support the business's current and future operational needs in areas such as management, financial stability reinvestment.
5) Familial	The plan should help to maintain family harmony and achieve family goals.

6) Emotional   An exit plan should address how you strive for peace of mind in your post exit life.

With these six areas in mind, it's possible to offer guidance on what a thorough exit plan looks like:

- An exit plan must be in writing. If it's all in your head, then should something happen to your head the plan will not be much help.

- A sound exit plan should clearly state your goals. Chapter Two will present the Seven Essential Questions of Exit Planning—a sound plan should help address those questions.

- Your plan should be reviewed by your accountant(s), attorney(s), financial advisor(s) and any other trusted advisor. Exit planning is a multi-disciplinary effort. How these advisors help you create and implement your plan is discussed later in the book.

- A helpful plan should use everyday vocabulary. Highly technical terms, complex charts and complicated concepts may hinder your ability to use and implement the plan.

- Expect your plan (and your advisors) to provide clear recommendations rather than just list options. The plan ideally includes specific and measurable action items and appropriate deadlines to implement each.

- Your plan must be current. Closely-held businesses change rapidly. You and your goals will likely change. Your advisors should help you keep your plan current. Plans older than one year may require careful review.

- A sound plan must address potential risks that may occur. Life throws you curve balls. You could die prematurely. Your hand-picked successor (child or key employee) could decide he or she does not want the business after all. Your business partner could demand you buy him out early. The well-designed plan anticipates relevant possibilities and maps out a course of action should you encounter one.

How to Use This Book

This book is divided into ten chapters grouped in three sections. The first section, Chapters One through Four, applies to all owners. These initial four chapters provide the foundation for your exit planning. After reading the first four chapters, you likely will have clearly defined exit goals and know which of the four possible exit strategies most likely applies to you.

The second section consists of Chapters Five through Eight. Each of these four chapters focuses on one of the four possible exit strategies. While you are welcome to read all four of these chapters, the book's format allows you to read only the one chapter that covers your likely exit strategy. Each of these chapters explores that specific exit strategy in greater detail, identifies common issues and suggests tactics and tools tailored to that exit strategy.

In the third section, Chapters Nine and Ten pull all readers back together again. The final two chapters address your plans for life after exit and suggest practical next steps for how to implement what you will have learned from this book.

Finally, many chapters share tactics and tools that may help you advance toward the end zone. In honor of Elmo Wright, these are categorized as plays for your Playbook. At the risk of extending the metaphor too far, just like a football coach you don't have to run every play in the book. Some of the nearly sixty plays will work better in specific situations or not be effective in others. Typically, you will consider running only those plays that best fit your needs. An Appendix at the end summarizes the entire Playbook for convenient reference.

Are you ready? Then: "Down!...Set!...Hike!"

Key Points:

- Exit planning not about some future transaction. It is the conscious effort to grow your business in a manner that efficiently converts ownership into personal financial freedom and peace of mind.

- Most owners are highly unprepared because they are waiting to get started. Sound exit planning can make your business better and your life better. Do not wait.

- The Baby Boomer age wave may flood the market with exiting owners over the next fifteen years, making exit success harder for unprepared owners.

2

The Seven Essential End Zone Questions

There are seven questions every business owner must consider and eventually answer to dance in the end zone. Your answers shape the entire exit planning process. Contrary to some approaches, one of the seven is not "What is my business worth?" A more careful examination reveals that, while this issue is important, other matters need to be addressed first before we determine the business's value. The Seven Essential End Zone Questions are:

1) When do you want to exit?

2) What is your likely exit strategy?

3) How much is your Exit Magic Number?

4) Where will it come from?

5) What risks do you face prior to exit?

6) What will you do in life after exit?

7) Who is your exit planning team?

Owners often initially struggle with these questions. Exit may seem too far away, the issues too complex or the choices too many. In our experience, answers are not difficult with the proper tools. Discussing and answering these seven questions takes you far down the path of preparing for the eventual exit.

Question #1: When Do You Want to Exit?

The first question asks when you want to exit from the business? In five years? Ten? At age 65? We start with "when" because how much time we have until your target exit date determines the tactics available to achieve your exit objectives. With less time generally fewer choices exist. It's another example of why exit planning needs to start now.

Before going further, what if you're an owner who never wants to exit? You love what you do too much and always see yourself working and leading your business. I've met many like you and your passion is a gift. There are several simple reasons why you still must address these questions:

- Nobody lives forever—at some point your business, employees, customers and others will have to go on without you. Most owners who are that passionate about their business care deeply about what happens to their business and employees when they are gone.

- While many owners aspire to work for a long time and not "retire" in the traditional sense of the word, keep in mind our definition of exit planning focuses on your financial freedom and not retirement. Financial freedom means that you do not *need* a paycheck; you can afford your desired lifestyle without any earned income. Most of the owners that I have met want to work as long as possible yet aspire towards achieving financial freedom.

- You may not always feel the way you do now. I have seen many owners change their mind. Within only a few years, the owner goes from wanting to work forever to desiring a quick exit. Many owners suffer from "irrational entrepreneurialism"—a passionate optimism that sustains their enthusiasm deep into working years. (If business owners were not irrationally entrepreneurial, they likely would never have started a closely-held business in the first place.) As a result, many owners do not gradually wind down toward an exit date as they age. Rather, they go over an emotional cliff—all is great today but within a short time they cross over a point and then want out.

The Rolling Ten Years

When asked about their ideal exit time frame, owners usually provide a target date expressed as a number of years from now, such as, "I want to exit in the next ten years." Using a range expressed in future years allows owners to innocently and often unconsciously perpetually roll forward their time frame, blurring the goal. Owners who answer this question with something like "in about ten years," do not change their answer to "in about nine years" twelve months later. We call this habit the Rolling Ten Years.

It showed up in our research. We asked nearly 450 owners when they want to exit. As you might expect, generally older owners have sooner ideal exit timeframes. However, an important insight came from the research:

Table 2-1: The Rolling Ten Years

Owner Age	Percentage of owners who ideally want to exit within the next 10 years
60 and older	72%
50 to 59	72%
40 to 49	63%
30 to 39	47%

Source: White Horse Advisors 2008 Survey of Closely-held Business Owners

You will note that among owners over age 50 and older, more than seven out of ten stated their ideal time frame was within ten years. Almost two of three, of owners ages 40-49 also said ten years, and nearly half of owners ages 30-39. The "ten year answer" keeps rolling forward from the owner's 30s all the way to the 60s.

Your response to the "When?" question should set a range for the earliest possible and latest desirable age. For example, you might like to exit not before age 55 and not any longer than age 60. Tighten the range as much as possible—no more than a five year spread is best. Setting a goal of between age 50 and 70 does not give much guidance. Using an ideal age range sets clearer expectations and eliminates the Rolling Ten Years bad habit. This approach also creates a healthy sense of urgency that time is not finite and sound planning needs to get started.

Question #2: What is your most likely exit strategy?

If the first essential question asks *"when?"*, then the second question asks *"how?"* For many owners, this is the hardest question. Yet it is essential because the answer identifies the issues and challenges you face, and the tactics to appropriately consider a successful exit.

Ben Franklin observed that death and taxes were two of life's few certainties. Allow me to add a third. Every owner must exit from his business, one way or another. Either during your lifetime or at death, your business will be given away, sold or liquidated. These three outcomes are not exit *strategies*. The word "strategy" implies a desirable result. Death is not a strategy! There are, in fact, four plausible exit strategies. It's important to identify as early as possible your most likely strategy that will take you down a clear path of what's needed to achieve a successful exit. The four exit strategies are:

1)   Pass to Family

2)   Sell to Outside Third Parties

3)   Sell to Inside Key Employees

4)   Planned Liquidation

Two important notes before we proceed. One, not all sales are equal. Selling your business to an outside party is a completely different process from selling it to your inside top employees. We differentiate between those two strategies because the issues, tactics are different as explained later in the book.

Second, Planned Liquidation does not mean failure. *Unplanned* liquidation could signify failure. Planned Liquidation implies that in a time and manner of your choosing, the business will be closed in an orderly way. Many highly successful enterprises have little value outside the owner's work ethic, talents and relationships. This is not an insult to the business but rather a testament to the owner's personal skills and achievements. Owners who intend to eventually close down the business still have an acute need to for exit planning; they do not need *succession planning* because transitioning to new management is not an issue. These owners must expect little value for their business at exit above the business's liquidation value. Owners pursuing Planned Liquidation must adopt a *current-cash* based approach to converting their business wealth rather than a *future-equity* based approach. As we will see, these owners are not alone. Contrary to much of the conventional wisdom, most closely-held business owners need to incorporate some current-cash based tactics into their exit planning and cannot afford to just sit back and wait for a future-equity based payday.

The Exit Strategy Decision Tree

At first, you may not know or be sure of your likely exit strategy. A process-of-elimination approach often helps identify the most likely exit strategy. While circumstances and your ultimate exit strategy may change, determining the most *likely* strategy helps you and your advisors consider tactics to maximize exit results. The Exit Strategy Tree starts with the following statement:

> I want family, who have the desire, ability and youth to succeed me, to one day own my company.

Do you agree or disagree with this statement? We start here because most owners with family members positioned to succeed them want the business to stay with family. If your answer to this statement is "Yes" then your likely exit strategy is to Pass to Family. Each of the four exit strategies uses a short, easy-to-remember (if borderline corny) descriptive term. Owners whose likely exit strategy is to pass the business to family are called *Passers*.

If you said "No" to the first statement, then you must select from the following three the statement that best fits your situation. You may have more than one that could fit, but approach this like the standardized tests many of us took in school—choose the answer that "best fits." Read them carefully, for each statement includes several important details. The first from the set of three reads:

> My business clearly offers to an outsider transferable value significantly above book (liquidation) value.

If this statement best fits, then you have the chance to sell your business to an outside party and be paid for its value as a going concern. In this case you are an *Outie*.

The second statement reads:

> My trusted employee(s) could now, or in the future with preparation, profitably run my business. They also have the desire to own my business and the youth to outlast me.

If this statement best fits your situation, then your likely exit strategy may be to sell to key employee insiders. You're an *Innie*. Note that there are several important parts to this statement. The employee(s) ideally is trusted, prepared, has the desire and will be young enough to take over. Remove any one of those factors and this may not be a viable option for you.

Oh Nuts – That Won't Work

I met Jerry when he was about 45 and owned a successful $10 million business he had founded about ten years earlier. Jerry reluctantly agreed to meet on the advice of his accountant. Less than three minutes into our lunch meeting he warned, "I don't need an exit plan. I have things all taken care of. I'm going to sell to my employees."

I asked him to tell me about them. He listed three or four people, all of whom he felt where talented workers and fine human beings. I congratulated him on assembling an excellent team. Then I asked him how old each person was. He said, "Well, Mary is in her early 40's I think, and Bob is a few years older than me. Andrew is about the same age as me, and Conrad is in his early 50's."

"Fine," I replied. "Jerry when did you say you wanted to exit?"

"In about ten years," he said.

"How old will these people be when you're 55?" I asked.

Jerry's ice tea glass was half way up to his mouth when I put this final question to him. He froze, and slowly put his glass down on the table.

"Oh nuts," he groaned. "That won't work. Ten years from now they'll all be thinking about retirement."

None of the previous statements may seem right for your business. The last statement to consider is:

None of the previous statements fit well. Most likely I will close my business in an orderly manner at the time of my exit.

In this situation your likely exit strategy may be Planned Liquidation. This owner must consider tactics that use the business's current cash to convert value along the way. In simple words, squeeze the business dry. If this is you, you are a *Squeezer*.

Determining whether you likely are a Passer, Outie, Innie or Squeezer is one of the most important steps in your exit planning. As you will see throughout this book, owners in the four different paths face four different sets of issues, risks and tactics. Knowing which type of business owner you are allows you to focus on only those tactics appropriate for your exit goals. Throughout the book we will clearly indicate how the issue or topic applies, or does not apply, to each of the four different strategies.

Question #3: How much is your Exit Magic Number?

Most owners want to achieve financial freedom, which means that *needing* a paycheck is high on your exit goals. You may choose to work after exit, and that work may generate additional income, but you do not need the earned income.

The Exit Magic Number is how much value you need to get from the business between now and your target exit date to achieve financial freedom. I will give some examples and review how this figure is calculated in a moment. However, note that the Exit Magic Number focuses on how much you **need** from the business, not what your business is worth. This is a different approach from most conventional approaches, which emphasize getting "maximum value" for the business. Getting maximum value is good and desirable, but may not be the most important issue. What if you succeed in getting "maximum value" but find you are unable to afford financial freedom? Is this a successful exit?

When "Maximum Value" is Below the Minimum

Dan, owner of a successful manufacturing business, received an unsolicited offer of $7 million for his business. After twenty years of sweating and sacrificing, the number was beyond his wildest expectations. He sold. After debt and taxes he ended up with $4 million in cash. At that point Dan and his accountant called us to analyze his annual needs and map out a plan for financial freedom. Dan was in his mid 50's, wanted to invest conservatively and maintain a lifestyle that was affluent but not excessive. The analysis showed Dan required about $4.5 million of capital to provide his desired annual income needs for life.

For most people, $4 million is not pocket change—Dan would never go hungry. But he was going to have to scale back his lifestyle, invest more aggressively than he was comfortable with, or find other sources of income. In other words, he was not financially free. The $7 million price may have been the "maximum value" for Dan's business, but Dan told us that if he knew how much he *needed* prior to exit, he might have changed his decision or negotiated different terms. At a minimum Dan would have avoided an unwelcome surprise of a $500,000 shortfall at the end of his long and successful career.

In effective exit planning, we want identify and be absolutely certain to achieve your Exit Magic Number. If you get anything above it, that is gravy. Before we go after "maximum value," we need to make sure we have the base need covered.

Calculating the Exit Magic Number

You will need some help calculating your Exit Magic Number, either from appropriate financial modeling software if you're comfortable with doing it yourself or from your financial advisors. Either way, the first step is to identify how much total capital is needed to support your income needs for life when you exit, taking into account investment results and inflation. For example, let's assume a business owner named Mary who is currently 45 years old wants to exit at age 60 with $200,000 of after-tax annual income in today's dollars for her lifetime. Mary assumes a life expectancy of age 85 so she will need the income for 25 years. Therefore, we need to calculate how big of a nest egg Mary will need to create $200,000 per year of income in today's dollars starting at age 60 while increasing the income each year to stay current with inflation. Let's assume for our purposes that this figure is about $5 million.*

The second step is to subtract from the total capital needed the amount of capital and income you expect to have *already available outside the business at the exit date*. Let's assume that Mary owns outside her business the commercial office building it leases. She believes the building's net equity will be $1 million by her exit date in fifteen years. With this potential $1 million already outside the business available for income (either by selling the building or by earning rental income) then her Exit Magic Number has fallen from $5 million to about $4 million.

> *Your Exit Magic Number is the total capital you require to achieve financial freedom minus the capital and income you already will have available outside of the business at the time of your exit.*

Your Exit Magic Number forecasts how much value you need to extract from your business leading up to and at your exit in order to achieve financial freedom. The more capital or income sources you have outside your business by the exit date, the lower your Exit Magic Number. If Mary sets up a profit sharing plan at her business, which she believes will reasonably grow in value to $500,000 by the time of her exit, her projected number falls to $3.5 million.

At its heart, the Exit Magic Number is a statement of how financially dependent you are on your business. A lower number is better and the ideal is zero. Remember that the Exit Magic Number is not about the value of the business. A higher number means you are more dependent on the value locked within your business to achieve financial freedom. Dependency usually makes exiting harder or more expensive at some point in the process. The owner who does not *need* any value from the business to achieve financial freedom enjoys the maximum flexibility; whatever you may get from the business at exit is gravy. Independence from the wealth locked in your closely-held business creates freedom to structure your exit in the most favorable manner to you, your family and your business. Said another way, it is usually easier to exit from a $5 million business with $5 million already

---

* Many owners are surprised at how large this figure can be. Properly considering inflation, taxes and market volatility can create surprisingly large amount. A million dollars is not what it once was.

in the personal bank account than to exit from a $10 million business with $0 in the bank.

Table 2-2: Mary's Exit Magic Number Calculation

Total capital needed at exit age 60	$5 million
Projected equity in commercial office building at age 60	- $1 million
Estimated value of profit sharing plan account at age 60	- $500,000
Projected Exit Magic Number at age 60	$3.5 million

An example of how a lower Exit Magic Number is advantageous involves taxes. Some owners have the chance to sell their business income tax free. Buyers may pay for your business using cash, debt or stock in the buyer's corporation if the buyer is another business. If stock is used, under a series of tax regulations it may be possible to treat the transaction as a stock "swap" rather than a sale. The selling owner ends up with the buyer's stock. Taking the buyer's stock may permit the exiting owner to defer or potentially even avoid paying capital gains, saving a small fortune in taxes. A funny thing about stock certificates however: they cannot pay the mortgage, buy groceries or put gas in the car. The more a selling owner *needs cash* from the business at exit in order to sustain financial freedom, the less ability he has to take advantage of this and other tax planning tactics. Dependency reduces flexibility.

Calculating and your Exit Magic Number clearly targets the *minimum* value you *need* from your business to achieve financial freedom. Your Number will change over time so monitor the figure not less than annually. The chart below provides some of the ways your Exit Magic Number may change:

Table 2-3: Factors Influencing Your Exit Magic Number

Your Number Will Increase If:	Your Number Will Decrease If:
You accelerate your exit timetable	You delay your exit timetable
Your desired income level at exit increases	Your desired income level at exit decreases

Your debt increases	Your debt decreases
Your assets or income sources outside the business decrease or grow at a slower rate than previously planned	Your assets or income sources outside the business increase or grow at a faster rate than previously planned

Going through the exercise is critically important. Lowering your Exit Magic Number creates more options and puts you in greater control of your exit plans. Chapter Four focuses on tactics to lower your Exit Magic Number.

Question #4: "Where will it come from?"

Once you know your Exit Magic Number, the next essential question is "Where will it come from?" The simplest answer is, of course, that it will come from your business. But *efficiently* converting your business into personal wealth rarely happens by accident. We encounter owners who believe if they take care of the business it inevitably will take care of them. If you sell your business, under current laws federal income taxes between the buyer and seller can easily total and exceed 69% of the total business purchase price. If you give your business to family, transfer taxes can reach and in some cases exceed 45%. More thoughtful planning is necessary to secure the greatest tax and other benefits. Unfortunately, too many owners ignore this issue until it is too difficult, if not too late, for implementing relevant tactics. To better tackle this essential question, we need to discuss The Dependency Dilemma.

The Dependency Dilemma

Most successful closely-held business owners have the majority of their personal wealth tied up in the business and its supporting assets. In the beginning you probably had to do this just to survive. As you grew, reinvesting solely in your business made perfect sense. The business was your most successful investment; it made little sense to invest in anything but the business. The faster your business grew, the more you wanted to reinvest back into it. That may still be true today. Reinvesting largely or exclusively back into your business increases your dependency on the value locked inside the business. In its most extreme form, your Exit Magic Number actually increases as you get closer to exit rather than falls. This happens when your standard of living (and the dollars required to support it) increases but the wealth you have outside the business stays flat or grows at a slower rate. We call this the Dependency Dilemma.

The Dependency Dilemma creates two problems. First, it is risky to have all one's eggs in one basket. You may be understandably confident in your ability to grow and protect your business investment. Yet any strategy where all the wealth is placed in one basket is inherently risky. You can get rich by investing in only one thing, but it may not be possible to stay rich that way.

The second problem is, as we have seen earlier, an owner with a high Exit Magic Number has less flexibility to pursue favorable tactics and tax benefits at exit. Even if the business is worth many tens or hundreds of millions and you have no doubt about affording your financial freedom, having comparatively little wealth outside the business makes exiting in a tax-efficient manner harder is most cases. When answering "where will it come from," the more diversified the resources then the more options available.

Current Cash Versus Future Liquidity

There are two approaches to converting business value into personal value—current cash and future equity. The two point to different courses of action. To make the point, assume at year end your CFO tells you the business has extra profits of $100,000 after taxes that you did not expect. Unless you want the money to go buy a new toy for personal use, what do you do with it? Do you deploy this current cash outside the business into some vehicle that creates wealth? Or do you invest it back into your business so that your future equity potentially increases? A combination of both?

Traditional succession planning focuses on the "liquidity event" that owners will experience at exit, assuming you will achieve your exit objectives largely or exclusively based on the business's future equity. In reality, many owners will never experience a liquidity event. Of the four exit strategies, Passers and Squeezers typically see little to no cash at exit. Often this is true for Innies. Even Outies may receive only a portion of their sale price in cash, the balance coming as installment payments or perhaps the buyer's stock if acquired by another business. Few owners can completely rely on future equity to meet their exit objectives. Most owners must also consider current-cash based methods to convert the business value into financial freedom and peace of mind.

Table 2-4: Current Cash vs. Future Liquidity

Exit Strategy	Likelihood of Future Equity	Need for Current Cash Based Approach
Passers	Low	High
Outies	Medium to High	Medium
Innies	Low to Medium	High
Squeezers	Low	High

The bottom line is that while the capital needed to fund your financial freedom and other exit objectives will come from the business, you probably cannot afford to just wait for the cash at exit, confident it will be enough despite taxes and other costs. Prudence and taxes should suggest that all owners consider using the tactics of their businesses to create wealth outside the business prior to exit. Chapter Four discusses these in depth.

Question #5: "What risks do you face prior to exit?"

As far as investments and assets go, a closely-held business is a different kind of animal. It's not like other assets such as real estate or publicly traded (marketable) stocks and bonds. Many of the characteristics are favorable—a successful business can create financial, emotional and personal rewards. Your personal talents and drive are key ingredients to the business performance, but matter little to the stock market. The entrepreneurial opportunity is what you may find so rewarding.

Like all investments and assets, however, your business is not immune from risk. Its risks are different from other types of assets too. Assume you owned three major assets: a closely-held business, a piece of real estate and a portfolio of marketable securities. If you should prematurely die or become seriously disabled, potentially your business could greatly suffer. It's not likely the real estate or marketable securities would drop in value. What if your business's top sales person quits and takes key customers to a competitor? Again, the real estate and securities will not suffer but the business could decline quickly. Unlike any other investment or asset, closely-held businesses by their very existence create risk.

Looking Through a Rose Colored Windshield

Kevin owned a profitable auto glass business in a mid-Atlantic state. About a quarter of his revenues consisted of preventative repairs to small scratches and cracks in before the entire windshield needed replaced. Auto insurance companies paid for these repairs, which made collections easy and led to additional work with these customers. Having reached his late 50's, Kevin contemplated selling and eventually hired a firm to market his business. The asking price was $8 million.

Shortly into the selling process, the legislature in Kevin's home state changed pricing and statutory guidelines for auto insurance. The new laws reduced the auto insurance companies' liabilities on windshield damages, removing the economic incentive for insurance companies to pay for preventative repairs. Kevin's gross revenues fell by nearly 50% overnight. He lost all of the windshield repair work and the follow-up business it generated. Kevin took his business off the market, and went back to work for many years trying to climb back up.

Of course it's impossible to eliminate all risks. A sound exit plan, however, identifies risks that could undermine your successful exit, and identify practical steps to address these risks. Chapter Three explores the risks Passers, Outies, Innies and Squeezers generally face and presents potential tactics to respond.

Question #6: "What will you do in life after exit?"

Many successful business owners feel understandable pride in their role and accomplishments. You've led an organization that has provided goods and services to meet clients' needs, created jobs that provide for families and even paid taxes (lots of taxes in many cases) that communities need for schools, hospitals and roads. Perhaps other than being a spouse and parent, much of your sense of self-worth is rooted in your identity as a business owner. Exiting without knowing what comes next in life can get you in trouble. As long as your health holds up, you probably have too much to give to do nothing that challenges you and rewards you. Rest and relaxation may be well deserved, but for many successful former-owners it quickly becomes not enough. The issue is not just about you. Exit may greatly change your relationships with family and close friends.

I Did Not Agree to Lunch Everyday

Jerome and Nancy were married for more than thirty years. We met with them for a routine review about a year after Jerome had exited from his large business via a public sale. During our meeting, we asked how they were. Jerome clearly could not be happier. He was in shorts and a golf shirt and playing 18 holes that same afternoon. He actually put his feet up on the conference table, stretched back and said, "I should have done this years ago."

Nancy patiently waited for Jerome to finish and then provided her answer. She said, "We've been married for more than thirty years. In our vows I promised 'in sickness and in health, for better or worse, until death do us part.' But you know, I never promised to do lunch every day."

She went on to explain to an increasingly surprised Jerome that she loved him very much and was thankful for his success and current relaxation. But she pointed out Jerome was not even 60 yet. She wanted to know what he was going to do with himself every day for the next 25 years, and did he really expect her to make him lunch every day?

Life is too unpredictable to know with certainty what's in store for you after exit. In many cases you may remain involved in your business or industry but in a different role. Asking and attempting to answer this question before you exit reduces the chance that you find yourself disappointed and regretful. Chapter Nine will explore this essential question of your life after exit in detail.

Question #7: "Who is your exit planning team?"

Exit planning is a team sport. You need to assemble a multidisciplinary advisory team that can address all of the elements of an exit plan. As discussed in the first chapter, exit plans must be sound from a tax, legal, financial, managerial, familial and emotional standpoint. Designing or implementing an exit plan without a competent team is a recipe for frustration and potential failure.

Most owners need on the team their accountant, attorney, financial advisor and spouse or other trusted family members. We refer to this as the Core Team. Your advisors must have experience relevant to your situation and exit strategy. (Your exit planning team is covered in Chapter Ten.)

Depending upon your situation, you and the Core Team may require additional expertise. For example, a business valuation expert may be needed to appraise the business's value. Your banker may play an important role, both to preserve existing lending arrangements or assist in new lending needs. Bonded companies such as contractors may consider including the surety bond agent on some level. If the company is to be sold, then an intermediary—often called a business broker, mergers and acquisition specialist or investment banker, may play a critical role. These individuals are considered the Support Team. The Support Team assists with a component of the exit plan and may not be required beyond their direct area of service and expertise. Ultimately, it is important to assemble and work with a team of advisors that have the skills, experience and intent to guide you through the complete process. Chapter Ten lays out a road map for you and your team on how to effectively work together, and where to get started.

Conclusion

Answering the Seven Essential End Zone Questions does not produce a comprehensive exit plan. Important details remain for you and your team to address. The questions determine much of your path to avoid spending time on issues, tactics or concerns not relevant in your situation. With these seven questions answered, you know where you likely need to go , by when, for what amount, how it may be created, what issues to consider and who will help you. At that point, we're marching down the field toward towards your future dance in the end zone.

Key Points:
- **With help from advisors, answer the Seven Essential End Zone questions to start your exit planning.**

- Identifying if you are a Passer, Outie, Innie or Squeezer spotlights the key issues you face and identifies tactics to meet your exit objectives.

- Your Exit Magic Number is the amount you need from your business to achieve financial freedom.

3

Risk Management Prior to Exit

Many successful owners see their business as a low risk asset. The business is an asset you have a high degree of control over. You probably have navigated the business through some rough waters on more than one occasion. You have a good team, provide superior products and services and don't take unnecessary risks. Despite inherent strengths and resiliency, even the best managed closely-held business can be a fragile venture:

- Closely-held businesses are usually less capable of weathering significant downturns in their industry or market due to their smaller size.

- Many closely-held businesses would suffer serious setbacks with the loss of a few or sometimes even just one top employee, customer or supplier.

- Your premature death or a serious disability can undermine or even wipe out your business's value.

- Serious disputes among co-owners can erode value or even break apart the strongest business.

Risk management is an essential component of exit planning because these and other threats create a double jeopardy for you. Anything that undermines the business puts not only your current profitable operations at risk but also threatens the future value you need from your business. Despite this, too many exit plans ignore risk management. It's not glamorous compared to other matters such as getting maximum value at sale or defeating high taxes. It may be difficult to make risk management a priority—you are a successful owner because you have taken risks, not because you "managed" them. But owners who address potential risks are better positioned to achieve their exit objectives whatever the future brings.

There are business risks outside the scope of this book: unfavorable economic trends, unforeseen technological developments, increased competition, etc. These threats are *leadership risks*, meaning the Chief Executive Officer of a business faces those issues whether he is an owner or not. Other risks are *ownership risks*, meaning they present direct threats to the business owner's goals. If you are both a CEO and owner, you may have to deal with both risk types. This book focuses on five common ownership risks:

1. The Risk of Under-Diversified Assets

Most owners have from 50%-90% of their personal net worth tied up in their closely-held businesses and its supporting assets. This creates risk— nearly all of your eggs sit in one basket. To borrow a saying from those who invest in the stock market, you can get rich by investing in only one stock but it's tough to stay rich that way. We discussed this risk in the Dependency Dilemma, which describes the tendency for successful owners to reinvest heavily inside their business, making them increasingly dependent on getting value out of the business at exit. (See Chapter Two.) This is probably the greatest risk for most owners. Because of its importance and with a variety of tools available to help, the entire next chapter is dedicated to this issue.

2. The Risk of Unwanted Co-Owners

There are many ways a portion of your business could find its way into unwanted hands:

- A co-owner dies and leaves his interest to his spouse or other heirs, leaving you with a new set of business partners

- A creditor could be awarded ownership after an asset dispute such a divorce

- A top employee that had been awarded or sold ownership later quits and starts or joins a competing business.

Any of these situations creates the potential for a large mess. Current business profitable operations may be interrupted. Legal disputes can arise. The present and future business value may be diminished. Few things can be as unpleasant as sharing your business with an unwanted co-owner. Your first line of defense against this risk is a buy-sell plan.

Playbook: Buy-Sell Plans

Buy-sell plans are perhaps the most widely recognized but least properly used risk management tool. At their core, buy-sell plans are two-way IOU's with a trigger attached. "Two-way" because two (or more) parties agree to a transaction involving the transfer of business ownership for consideration. A "trigger" exists because the arrangement specifies when one party is required to buy and another party to sell interest in that business. For example, if your business partner dies then you must buy his interest from his heirs, and they must sell his interest to you. A buy-sell agreement is a legal document. Owners commonly use tools such as life and disability insurance to fund the agreement's financial obligations. Together, the legal document and the funding vehicle make up a *buy-sell plan*.

The common thinking is only businesses with multiple owners need a buy-sell. If you're currently the only owner in your business, you may still consider a buy-sell plan with another party such as a top employee to protect against diminishment of the business's value upon your personal death or disability. This arrangement, a "one-way" buy-sell plan, is discussed in Chapter Seven.

Buy-Sell Plans Purposes and Advantages

Much has been written about buy-sell plans and your advisors probably can discuss them in great detail, but it's important that you understand their basic purposes and advantages. Well designed buy-sell plans may accomplish all of the following:

- Protect against an owner selling or transferring his interest in the business to an unwanted third party, either intentionally or unintentionally

- Establish a price or method for appraising the business before a triggering event occurs, reducing potential disagreement and divisiveness

- Help preserve the business's value should an owner prematurely die or suffer a serious disability

- Provide reassurance to creditors, employees and other parties for the orderly continuation or dissolution of the business upon a triggering event

- Prevent against stock in an S corporation being sold or transferred to an ineligible individual or entity

- Assure continuation of general and limited partnerships upon the death of a partner.

Questions the Buy-Sell Should Answer

A thorough buy-sell legal agreement must address a wide range of issues. Some of the most important include:

1. How Will the Business Be Valued?

With publicly traded companies, business value is largely determined by the stock price in the open market. Closely-held businesses lack an open market, making valuation difficult and extremely subjective. In good times, different parties can examine the same business and reach radically different conclusions. In times of transition or unexpected hardship, differing opinions on the closely-held business value can derail the strongest exit plan. Consider with your advisors how your buy-sell agreement should determine the business value.

Some agreements simply call for an appraisal of the business upon a triggering event. The agreement may predetermine who will do the valuation, such as your regular accounting firm if they do business appraisals. In the event of a dispute, the plan may call for multiple appraisals to be conducted and the results combined in some manner. In my experience, I am not in favor of an agreement that first calls for an appraisal. It's on owners to make other decisions if we have no idea what the business might be worth. For example, if you want to purchase life insurance to fund the buy-sell upon an owner's death, it's difficult to know how much insurance you need if you don't know today an approximate business value. Appraisals often work best as a backup arbitration mechanism in the event that another valuation method has failed.

Rather than just calling for an appraisal upon a triggering event, a buy-sell agreement can specify how the business will be valued by using either a *formula* or a *fixed price*. Formulas tend to be more commonly used. For example, the agreement might specify that the business is worth "two times last year's gross profits" or "four times EBIT (earnings before interest and taxes)." A formula's primary advantage is the resulting number changes as the business changes over time. Proceed with caution however as formulas are often too vague and leave the door open for disagreement. Consider the formula "two times last year's gross profits." Does "last year" mean the last fiscal year, calendar year or most recent 12 month period? Does "gross profits" mean reported profits, or should profits be adjusted to add back excessive compensation and other expenses that many successful closely-held business owners use to reduce taxable profits? If you use a formula, clearly define it. Keep your notes on how you selected that formula in case there is uncertainty or disagreement in the future about what the formula means and how it was derived.

Value Volatility

Larry and Sherry equally own a construction business. When we met them their existing buy-sell plan used a formula of "three times book value" to set the business's value. Their business's book value experiences huge swings up and down over the course of the calendar year as their construction projects move from start towards completion. Three times book value could be $20 million in one month but more than $32 million just a few months later. Depending on the time of the year the funding obligations under this valuation method increased and fell by more than fifty percent! The owners and their attorney revised the buy-sell formula to adjust for volatility in the business' financial statements by specifying that the book value should be determined on the final day of last complete fiscal year.

Another challenge with using a formula to value the business is it often creates a false sense of security—the buy-sell plan is not reviewed frequently enough because the owner believes that the formula accommodates his ever-changing business. Formulas need to be updated. Macroeconomic issues, industry trends, company financials, owner objectives and other factors can erode the soundness of a formula that fit well in the past. Work with your advisors and review it every year.

The last method to set the business value in a buy-sell agreement is to fix a specific price in the agreement. For example the legal document might state, "The business is worth $10 million." This method's advantage is the clarity it offers at the time the document is drafted and signed. Unlike formulas, a fixed price leaves no room for debate or confusion—the business is worth ten million dollars and no cents. The main disadvantage of course is things change and owners and advisors may fail to keep the specified amount current. An out-of-date price can cause a lot of trouble.

Western Showdown Backfire

Two owners, Carl and Bill, had in place a five-year old buy-sell agreement which fixed the price of the business at $3 million. But during the last several years the business had tripled in size and profitability. However during the same time period their relationship deteriorated to the point where the Carl wanted to force Bill to sell to him.

Invoking a buy-out clause in their buy-sell agreement commonly called a "western showdown," Carl demanded that Bill buy him out. The clause mandates that if one owner demands a sale, the other owner must purchase at that price, or if not then must sell at that price. It's a "western showdown" because only one owner is left standing. Carl failed to take into account the out of date value in their agreement, leaving Bill unable to afford to buy the business and thus forced himself to sell.

Instead Bill easily borrowed sufficient funds based on the increased size and strength of the business and bought out Carl for the $3 million price specified in the buy-sell.

If you use a fixed price, create a specific time each year to update the figure, such as when preparing and reviewing your business's year-end financial statements. Also, consider putting an expiration date in the legal agreement after which time an arbitration process is mandated if the price has not been updated. This protects against a very old number coming back to bite somebody.

2. What are the Triggering Events?

Death

Everybody recognizes the threat of premature death. In nearly twenty years I have never seen a buy-sell agreement that forgot to address an owner's expected death. In most cases the buy-sell plan stipulates that upon the death of an owner, his interest in the business will be purchased by the remaining owners or by the business itself. This arrangement protects the remaining owners and provides the deceased owner's heirs with cash so their life may go on without being financially tied to the business.

Disability

In contrast to the universally recognized risk of premature death, I have read many buy-sell plans that fail to address an owner's serious disability. Most people do not expect to get disabled. Successful owners are often hard-working, dedicated individuals who cannot see themselves incapacitated from an accident or illness. In fact, the likelihood of a long term disability occurring is actually greater than the risk of dying prior to age 65 in most cases.

Should a serious disability occur, the ownership and financial picture is often more difficult to manage than upon an owner's death. Usually nobody wants to terminate the disabled owner's paycheck during the disability even though the business may be suffering from the loss. Uncertainty over the disabled owner's ability to recover can delay important business decisions. Addressing the risk of disability is no less important than properly planning for the contingency of a premature death.

Retirement

In this happier situation, buy-sell agreements should specify procedures for purchasing a retiring owner's interest in the business, The agreement should address the terms, price, timing, funding sources and other important considerations. The agreement also may specify how retirement before normal age may be handled, often overlooked. For example, if a co-owner wanted to leave the business before normal retirement age, should he receive the same buyout price as if he had stayed longer? Some co-owners agree among themselves to discount the buyout price if a co-owner chooses to leave early to acknowledge that the business probably has suffered a setback with that person's premature loss combined with the burden of an early buyout.

Other Lifetime Transfers

A well drafted buy-sell agreement also protects other scenarios that may result in unwanted co-owners. This may occur if an owner divorces and the non-working spouse seeks a portion of the business in the divorce settlement. Owners additionally may want to avoid a co-owner unilaterally selling or giving his business interests to another party without consent. Toward this end, the legal agreement often includes a "first right of refusal" provision that puts each owner first in line to acquire another owners' business interests.

Failure to Perform Duties

Many owners are also key employees in their own businesses. If an owner fails to perform his responsibilities or engages in activities that potentially harm the business, this could seriously erode the business's value or profitability.

Walker's Walkabout

Henry and Walker were fifty-fifty owners of a large steel supply business. Revenue and profits had been strong for several years after many early years of sweat and sacrifice. The business's success finally allowed both owners to scale back to forty hour weeks and take regular vacations.

One day Henry noticed that Walker was taking longer and longer vacations. Henry was glad they both could enjoy the time away, but he wondered how much time was too much. When Walker returned he casually asked him about this. Walker laughed and said "Isn't it great? You should too Henry. We've earned it." Henry thought perhaps Walker was right and forgot about it.

A month later, Henry noticed Walker was absent for a standard semi-annual meeting of the whole firm. He knew Walker had been on vacation, but he had expected him back. Henry asked Walker's secretary, who seemed surprised to tell him that Walker had called last week and said he was on a "walkabout" and might not be back for a few weeks. Upon further investigation Henry realized his partner had been away half of the last seven months. Walker's department continued performing well, but a number of long term strategic projects had fallen far behind schedule.

When Walker returned Henry insisted that they discuss this issue. Walker quickly grew defensive, saying he had worked too hard to not enjoy the time away. Henry agreed, but said perhaps they should change their compensation arrangements if Walker wanted that much time away—up to this point they had always taken the same salary and split the business profits equally. Walker grew angry at this suggestion said he would oppose any such move.

Their impasse continued until finally Walker did not come in for nearly two months straight. By then Henry consulted with his lawyer. The buy-sell agreement addressed an owner's death and other situations, but it did not address what to do if an owner simply stopped working. Henry's lawyer said he could try and fire Walker, but there were no written job descriptions or compensation plans so Henry risked a lawsuit and possible fight over the business. As fifty-fifty owners, neither had final authority over the other. Henry was stuck and Walker was on walkabout. At the time of this writing, that is where they remain today.

3. Where Will the Money Come From?

When a buy-sell is triggered a financial obligation to purchase an interest in the business is created. This can be a significant amount of money due with little to no advance notice. Most owners and advisors recognize the benefits purchasing insurance to cover a death or disability. Insurance is the only funding tool that can provide the cash—income tax free—immediately when needed.* There are several important considerations when designing and implementing an insurance portfolio:

---

* Note that life insurance premiums for buy-sell plans and in most other situations are not deductible for personal income tax purposes while the death benefits are usually income tax free. Disability insurance premiums may be deducted for income tax purposes in many cases, but doing so creates a benefit subject to income taxes. If you do not deduct the disability insurance premiums, then any benefits paid are usually income tax free. Discuss with your advisors not deducting disability premiums because the few dollars you save today puts thousands of future dollars at risk to income taxes when you least want to pay them. There are fees, costs and possible restrictions associated with life insurance.

- Maintain sufficient insurance to meet the financial needs. We commonly see insufficient coverage usually because the business has grown in value since the buy-sell plan was established or last reviewed. Review annually the insurance need and update as necessary. Consider purchasing slightly more insurance than may be exactly required to create room for anticipated growth in the business value.

- Do not give up if an owner is uninsurable. Occasionally one or more owners are too old or have medical conditions that preclude cost-effective coverage. In a multi-owner business, one owner's advanced age or poor health should not prevent securing proper coverage on the others. Also, challenge the financial advisor or insurance agent to be creative. Consider using group insurance plans rather than individual policies as they may offer less strict medical requirements. Group insurance may not be able to provide the full amount needed, but some insurance is usually better than none.

- Do not neglect disability insurance. Rarely do we encounter a buy-sell plan with adequate disability insurance. Disability insurance premiums may be more expensive than life insurance, in part because the risk is higher. Owners also see disability as an "if" rather than "when" and resist implementing the coverage. It is important to remember that dying *before exit* is also an "if" rather than "when."

- The legal agreement should stipulate how the buy-out is to be handled if insurance is insufficient, such as setting terms for an installment purchase. Verify that the agreement also instructs for the disposition of unused insurance policies after the buy-out is triggered.

Triggering events other than death or disability present a different challenge—there's no insurance to buy. In these cases, the buy-sell agreement often stipulates a buy-out over time to allow the business and remaining owners to cash flow the required payments. Consult with your advisors and devise a payment schedule that is appropriate for any foreseeable scenario.

4. Who Will Be the Buyer?

There are two basic types of buy-sell agreements: entity-purchase[*] and cross-purchase agreements. The primary difference is who, or what, buys the interest. With an entity-purchase agreement, the business (the entity) is the buyer. Under a cross-purchase agreement, the remaining owners are the buyers.

A number of important pro's and con's exist with each method. For example, the income tax ramifications may be quite different if the business interest is bought by the business or purchased by individual owners. Attorneys, accountants and financial planners can attend entire workshops comparing the two methods and identifying scenarios where one is a better fit than the other. Trying to pick the ideal method years or even decades before a triggering event occurs is difficult. It also makes little sense when an alternative exists.

The alternative is commonly called wait-and-see buy-sell agreement. Under this method, the legal agreement does not predetermine who or what will be the buyer—the agreement will "wait and see." The legal document usually accomplishes this by giving the business a first option to purchase the interest within a narrow window of time such as 30 days. If this time period expires with no purchase, then the option shifts to specified individuals such as remaining owners to make the purchase. If these individuals do not purchase the interest within the second time period, then usually the agreement concludes that the third and final step is the business must purchase the interest. The wait-and-see sequence (easy to remember as Business-Owner-Business or B.O.B) gives the owners and advisors flexibility to determine the best course of action upon a triggering event.

Partnership Buy-Sell Plans

As the number of owners grows, buy-sell planning becomes more complex. More owners produce a less homogenous group in age, health, exit goals and other factors. Purchasing life and disability insurance coverage gets more difficult and expensive. For example, under a cross purchase buy-sell agreement the number of life or disability insurance policies required increases exponentially as the owner count increases. A formula, N x (N-1), calculates the potential number of policies:

---

[*] Also widely called stock redemption agreements because, before the common use of non-corporate entities such as LLCs, most closely-held businesses were corporations with stock. If the business entity purchases the stock this is a stock redemption.

Table 3-1: Policies Required Under Cross Purchase Agreements

Number of Owners	Number of Insurance Policies Required
2	2
3	6
4	12
5	20

To streamline buy-sell plans for multiple owner businesses, a separate legal partnership may be established to own the insurance policies. If an owner dies or becomes disabled, insurance proceeds are paid to the partnership. With the funds in the partnership, the remaining owners may execute the terms of the buy-sell agreement. The partnership restores the simplicity of one insurance policy per owner, helps keep the insurance policies in a single location and preserves any potential favorable tax planning procedures upon a triggering event.* The partnership may be combined with a wait-and-see legal agreement to provide maximum flexibility.

Common Mistakes with Buy-Sell Plans

Buy-sell plans are complex tools and it is easy to make mistakes. Owners and their advisors should take care to avoid the following three common errors:

1) Make sure the buy-sell, if triggered, does not generate an undesirable result. This can occur if the owner and advisors have not closely examined what would happen upon a triggering event.

The Stock Redemption Shuffle

All-Star Services Inc. had a buy-sell plan for its five owners that mandated, upon a triggering event, shares would be redeemed back by the business. The business was owned in the following manner:

---

* The life insurance death benefit is income tax free to the business if the business, at the time of purchase, had met the requirements of Internal Revenue Code 101(j) including providing the insured with advance notice, obtaining the insured's prior consent to be insured and meeting insured's executive income requirements.

• Owner A founded the company and owned 40% of the stock
• Owner B owned 30%
• Owners C, D and E each owned 10%

Under the agreement, if Owner A's stock were redeemed then Owner B would receive a controlling position because B would then own 50% of the *outstanding* stock. If B's stock was redeemed, A would be left owning 57% of the outstanding stock. When this possibility was pointed out, Owners C, D and E objected to the possibility that a single owner could control a majority of the business. Their attorney rewrote the agreement to a provide flexibility against this unintended outcome.

2) Include all the business entities and important assets. Owners often divide their business enterprise into multiple entities for operational advantages, estate planning and creditor protection. Buy-sell agreements written for the main operating business often fail to include these peripheral entities.

But What About the Building?

Lynda and Diane were equal owners of a successful real estate brokerage firm. They had implemented a buy-sell plan for their S corporation. Later, they purchased a commercial building for their business to occupy and set up a separate LLC to own the property. The building was in an ideal location and nearly doubled in value within several years. Lynda subsequently died. Diane assumed she would purchase Lynda's half of the building along with the business. However, the buy-sell plan only governed the real estate business and not the LLC which held their building.

Diane approached Lynda's heirs but they would only sell at an above market price given rising real estate market. Diane could not afford to pay the price they wanted, so Lynda's heirs began investigating selling their half to another party. Before long Diane was forced to move her business altogether and the valuable building was sold.

3) Confirm in writing that any life and disability insurance policies have the correct owner and beneficiary. If a death or disability happens and the insurance funds are paid to the wrong person or entity, it can be a tax and legal nightmare. We work with a business that had four owners and nine life insurance policies in place. The business's operating entity was a regular C corporation, but a partnership had been created along the way to own all of the insurance policies. Our audit of the insurance portfolio found only two of the nine policies properly owned inside the partnership. Should one of those owners have died, the funds would have ended up in the wrong place and potentially subjected their C corporation to adverse tax treatment under alternative minimum tax (AMT) rules.

Buy-Sell Plans are an Ongoing Process

Many owners spend valuable time and money to implement a sound buy-sell plan, only to put everything into a file cabinet and forget about it. Things change. Upon a triggering event, you don't want to find yourself saying, "I did not know the agreement still said this...The company is not worth that...We can't use that formula anymore...What about the other business we own?"

Buy-sell plans are easy to file and forget. Review the buy-sell agreement and its funding mechanisms once per year. An effective habit is to review the agreement each year when you meet with your advisors to review the business's year-end financial statements. It only takes a few minutes, your advisors will already be in the room, and you will have recent financial information to review and discuss how the business's potential value has changed. The business and your exit plan may be at stake.

3. The Risk of Opposing Agendas

This risk applies to businesses with multiple owners. If you are your business's sole owner, and expect to remain so, consider skipping this section.

Co-owners of the same business often assume that their individual exit goals are identical to, or at least compatible with, their co-owners' goals. In my experience this is often not the case. Two or more owners of the same business often have different and even opposing agendas. (For simplicity, we will make the assumption that you have just one co-owner with you unless otherwise noted.) For example, you and your co-owner may want to exit at different time periods. You may have different preferred exit strategies: you may be an Outie and he an Innie. You and your co-owner may have greatly different Exit Magic Numbers, which can leave you in direct conflict over how you achieve a successful exit.

What a Difference a Decade Makes

Aaron, 62 and Nate, 52 founded their technology business nineteen years earlier and owned it equally. Their business had grown into a local market leader and was highly profitable. One day a national competitor called with an all-cash offer to buy their business. It was an attractive price relative to their business size and earnings. After carefully reviewing the offer, Aaron was ecstatic and ready to sell, but Nate was ready to say no and go back to work.

The problem was the co-owners had vastly different Exit Magic Numbers. Because Aaron was ten years older, he needed less money to achieve financial freedom. In addition, Aaron's wife had accumulated a large retirement nest egg from her job, further reducing Aaron's Exit Magic Number. As a result of these differences, if they sold the business for the amount offered then Aaron could live happily ever after but Nate would need to go find a job. Unable to reach agreement, they eventually lost the offer and found themselves stuck.

Co-owners with opposing agendas can find themselves unintentionally upsetting or blocking each other's ability to happily and successfully exit, even in the most harmonious business relationships. It's not a question of right and wrong, but rather of potentially incompatible goals. You and your co-owner need to address this risk as early in the process as possible.

Playbook: Compare Your Seven Essential Questions

The most effective tactic to reduce this risk is to compare your respective answers to the Seven Essential Questions. A candid conversation will reveal where you are in alignment and where you may face opposing agendas. For example, comparing your ideal exit ages will identify if you and your co-owner have similar time horizons, or need to discuss a staggered exit. Comparing your Exit Magic Numbers will reveal under what scenarios one owner may exit to achieve financial freedom, but the other cannot. Note that the Exit Magic Number is particularly effective in this situation because it does not reveal the type of specific personal financial information that business partners commonly would not reveal. Sharing responses to the rest of the Essential Questions would contribute to a high level of mutual understanding. If helpful, rely on your advisors to facilitate the conversation and comparison.

Playbook: Create Multiple Exit Plans

Co-owners of the same business often fall into the trap of believing they have to exit at the same time and in the same manner, especially if you started the business together or are similar in age. In multiple owner businesses, often the need arises for multiple exit plans. There is no reason to attempt to meet all owners' needs using the same strategies and tactics. For example, if one owner intends to exit far earlier than the other, the first owner may sell to the second (making the first an Innie) while the second may identify a different likely exit strategy. This tactic may be especially helpful if one owner has a successor family member working in the business and the other does not. The potential still exists for opposing agendas, but they are easier to work out with sufficient time to identify and implement solutions. Last minute planning rarely brings success with multiple owner businesses.

4. The Risk of Losing You

As of today you may be one of or even the most valuable employee within your business. Even if you have built a highly successful and effective management team that runs your business, should something happen to you the business's value may nosedive: your management team, customers, lenders and suppliers may become nervous about the business's future and leave. In an extremely short time your business legacy may be lost and your family deprived of the business's value. Later in this book, we will discuss how to build your business so you are not its most valuable employee in order to successfully exit. At this point, we need to recognize the risk that your premature death or serious disability can compromise or even obliterate the business's value. Any sound exit plan must address the risk of something happening to you.

Playbook: Maintain Adequate Insurance

Part of the risk of losing you is managed through sound personal financial strategies, especially adequate life and disability insurance. While it's usually not difficult to locate a competent personal financial advisor, there are some important details when addressing the needs of closely-held businesses and their owners. If you own life insurance, generally own it outside of the business. This is a common mistake. If you should die and your family wants to put dollars back into the business they easily can. If you die and the dollars are paid directly into the business it may be hard to get those dollars out: the bank or other lenders may pressure the surviving owners to keep the dollars in the business, other surviving owners may want the dollars, or depending on your type of business and tax situation the insurance proceeds may be partially taxable if paid to the business. As an alternative, own the insurance personally or consider setting up an irrevocable life insurance trust to keep the insurance proceeds removed from estate taxes.

Owners (and their financial advisors) often address the risk of premature death but discount or ignore the risk of a serious disability because death is inevitable but disability is only possible. That logic is flawed. The risk we are addressing is the owner dying *while still an owner*, which is only a possibility. In most cases the risk you become disabled before normal retirement age is as great as or greater than the risk of death before normal retirement age. To address the risk of disability, start with sound personal insurance. Business owners also may consider a formal, written disability plan. Sometimes called Qualified Sick Pay Plans, they protect your ability to deduct income payments to you (or other employees should you include them) if you become disabled. Otherwise, the IRS may attempt to disallow the income tax deduction on payments made to you while you were not working. Be realistic about your business's ability to pay you if you became seriously disabled. Many owners complain about how they cannot get away enough, yet when they are looking at a disability insurance premium they rationalize "Oh, I don't need this. My business will just continue to pay me," as if it can indefinitely run on autopilot.

Playbook: Emergency Guidance Letter

One of the simplest and most effective risk management tools should something should happen to you is an Emergency Guidance Letter. This is your chance to let family and top employees know what to do if you can't. We rarely meet owners who have this device yet if something happens it can be as important as any insurance policy.

To draft your letter, consult with your advisors and devise simple but clear guidance on these and any other issues you feel are important. Try to remember that you cannot anticipate every scenario or issue—provide broad guidelines and trust in your family, employees and advisors to help and do the right things.

1) In your absence, who can be given the responsibility to continue and supervise business operations, financial decisions and client relations?

2) How will top employees be compensated for their time and, most importantly, for their commitment to continue working until the emergency is over? (Consider suggesting a "stay bonus" paid to employees if they remain to work through the emergency or if necessary an ownership transition.)

3) What should happen to the business at your death or if you are not capable of deciding?

4) What advisors should be consulted in the event of an emergency?

5) Where are important business and personal legal documents that may need to be reviewed in the event of an emergency? Who should review them?

Drafting and keeping current a letter which answers these questions could literally save your business if something happened to you. This may be another unglamorous risk management tactic, but you've worked too hard not to consider this simple but effective tool.

Playbook: Powers of Attorney

While a detailed discussion of estate planning is beyond the scope of this book, a document called a power of attorney is commonly used in estate planning and also effective in exit planning risk management. A power of attorney gives somebody else authority to make legally binding decisions on your behalf if you are unable to do so. For example, if you are in a car accident and fall into a coma, you may authorize one or more people to make business decisions that only you could otherwise make. A *general* power of attorney may be established to give broad powers to someone such as a spouse. A *specific* power of attorney may give more limited authority for somebody such as a trusted top employee.

Dealing with Wilson's Wipeout

Whenever Wilson would go for long motorcycle ride, his wife Sharon would say to him, "Please don't wipe out. I love you and I'd have no idea what to do with your business." Wilson was the sole owner of a restaurant chain worth $50 million.

Wilson's chief operating officer, Phil Preston, had been with him for twenty years. He knew the business inside and out. Wilson and Sharon trusted Phil in all manners. Wilson and his attorney implemented a specific power of attorney that would authorize Phil to make most major business decisions should Wilson die or become seriously disabled. They also implemented a compensation plan that would kick in at that time, creating a large stay bonus for Phil to keep in shape until it could be sold. After this was in place, Wilson observed that Sharon still told him to not to wipe out because she loved him, but at least the second part of her concerns had been addressed.

Playbook: One-Way Buy-Sell Plan

In this arrangement, you enter into a buy-sell agreement with a top employee to purchase your business should you die or become disabled. The buy-sell agreement is "one-way" in that it only triggers if something happens to you, not the employee. Everybody potentially benefits from this arrangement. You are assured that you or your family will receive full value for the business should something happen to you. Your employee has the opportunity to protect his job and continue the business legacy. This tool is discussed further in Chapter Seven: The Innie's Game Plan.

5. The Risk of Losing a Key Employee

Within many businesses, a few highly experienced and talented employees drive growth and profits. The unexpected loss of one or more top employees can seriously disrupt both current business results but also future exit plans. Despite their value, top employees often receive little specialized planning to protect against unexpectedly losing their services. Businesses spend thousands of dollars insuring buildings, property, cash, inventory and other assets. Yet good employees usually are legally and financially free to walk away or be lured away by competitors, taking with them invaluable information and relationships.

Owners' complacency usually stems from a mix of confidence in their employees' sense of loyalty, belief that top people could not make more somewhere else and simple denial that a valued employee could get sick or prematurely die. These are dangerous assumptions to make. Key employees may be highly loyal but are also highly marketable. Competitors can go after your top people. Talented employees can defect to start their own businesses. Nobody is invulnerable to serious illness, accident or premature death. Owners are wise to take reasonable efforts to reduce the risk of losing any employee whose loss would set back the business.

She's Key to Me

Who is a "key employee?" While obvious candidates are senior managers and top sales people, ultimately it is up to the owner. Years ago we asked the owner of an aviation service company if he had any key employees. Without hesitation he pointed out his open office door to his young administrative assistant. Curious, I asked why a younger and not highly paid clerical employee would be so important to him. He replied, "She's key to me. If she left I'd have to work more than I want to. I'd have the hire somebody new, and that person might not be as trustworthy. It's not worth it to me." Key employees are valuable however you define value.

There are three ways that an owner may unexpectedly lose a key employee:* death, disability or defection. Any of these "Three D's" can take a top employee away from your business. Owners have a number of tactics available to reduce this risk.

Playbook: Key Employee Life Insurance

Key employee life insurance protects the business should the insured employee die while working. In its purest form, key employee life insurance is designed to protect the company; the employee has no benefits from the

---

* Retirement is not an unexpected loss in most circumstances (unless the employee won the lottery). If you have to fire your key employee, I would argue that the employee was no longer a *top* employee but you had just not learned this yet.

policy.* If term life insurance is used, consider selecting a policy with a level premium that extends at least until your target exit age. For example, if your likely exit age is within ten years, then consider a term life insurance policy with level premiums for at least ten and perhaps fifteen years. That way the coverage will last until your exit age with a little room to spare. While there are a variety of methods to calculate how much insurance is prudent, most owners simply pick a reasonable amount that would provide an infusion of cash sufficient to hire and train a quality replacement should this person die.

Key employee life insurance has one drawback—it often creates complacency that the risk of losing a top employee has been fully addressed. Out of the Three D's, premature death may be the least likely to occur. A simple life insurance policy payable to the business has no impact against reducing the risk of disability or defection prior to the owner's exit.

Ownership in Your Business—To Share or Not to Share?

To reduce the risk of a key employee defecting, many owners consider giving or selling some of the business to their key employees. There are potential advantages of sharing ownership in your business: it can help retain the employees and motivate them to grow the business's value. However, sharing ownership is fraught with difficulties and potential problems; in my experience, it backfires as often as it succeeds. If it backfires, your ability to successfully exit may be jeopardized.

While the key employee may talk about wanting to own some of the business, often when you closely examine the situation the employee wants the rewards of ownership but not the risks. As you undoubtedly know, ownership in a closely-held business is not risk-free. Is this employee willing to personally guarantee the bank debt as you have? Is this employee willing to skip a paycheck if cash becomes tight as you probably have at some point? Is this employee willing and able to share the insomnia that comes with actual ownership?

Thankfully, there are other tools to retain and reward your top employees that do not involve sharing actual ownership.† They have a variety of names such as "synthetic stock" or "phantom stock" plans. In

---

* Under the Pension Protection Act of 2006, specific provisions apply regarding notifying and gaining consent from key employees to purchase life insurance. The regulation also sets specific guidelines on when any death benefits paid to the business will be income tax free.

† Note that at this point the goal usually is to retain, reward and motivate one or more top employees. We will examine how to sell the business to top employees in Chapter Seven.

general, these devices create a potential future cash reward to put "golden handcuffs" on your top employees without involving actual ownership in your business.

Table 3-2: Sharing Minority Ownership with Key Employees

Potential Advantages	Potential Disadvantages
Employee may be compelled to stay for the long term	Employee gains legal right to see business financial statements, books and records
Employee may be motivated to grow the business's value	May complicate your personal income tax, estate and retirement planning
Employee may come to appreciate the full risks of business ownership	May establish a precedent for other employees to expect the opportunity for ownership
	Dilutes your ownership position
	May require you to share profits in proportion to ownership
	Employee's personal difficulties (creditors, divorce) may threaten the business
	Employee's exit goals may be different from and contradict your goals

---

Playbook: Golden Handcuffs Plans

Imagine if you could handcuff your top employees to the business for as long as needed. Using iron chains is not possible, but chains made of gold are possible. Compensation programs that create cash incentives for the employee to stay are informally called Golden Handcuffs plans. These plans reward a valued employee for remaining and performing for the very long term by offering a significant cash reward payable only at a later date, ideally no earlier than this employees' retirement or your target exit age.

Golden Handcuffs plans commonly consist of a written agreement and a funding vehicle. The agreement specifies the potential benefits to the key employee and the criteria for achieving those benefits. As for funding the future promises, the business has no legal obligation to set aside any funds and may pay the benefits out of operating profits. However, many owners set aside at least some funds for the future promise for a variety of reasons, not least of which to demonstrate to the employee a serious commitment to fulfill the business's end of the bargain. Golden Handcuffs' plans may accomplish the following:

- Motivate the employee to stay for the long term without sharing ownership in the business

- Hand pick which employees to include

- Customize the future financial promise to the situation

- Require a long term vesting schedule designed to reduce risk the employee defects prior to the owner's likely exit date

- Design a funding strategy that minimizes the business owner's outlay and even creates the potential for total recovery of costs if desired.

Golden Handcuffs plans create these advantages largely because they are *non-qualified* employee benefit plans. *Qualified* employee benefit plans, such as 401(k) retirement plans, generally must comply with numerous federal laws including the requirement to include all eligible employees.* Non-qualified plans intentionally do not comply with many of these regulations in order to include only specific employees and create very long term incentives for them to stay.† A downside with Golden Handcuffs and other non-qualified plans is the business does not get an income tax deduction as long as the business holds back the money, and withholding the money is exactly what retains the employee for the long term. When the employee finally receives the compensation, then the business usually realizes an income tax deduction equal to the compensation paid. There are funding tactics however, to restore some of the tax attractiveness, but holding onto top people may be immeasurably more valuable to the business compared to the tax deduction. Golden Handcuffs plans have many variations, but commonly include the following components:

The Future Cash Benefit

The core of a Golden Handcuffs program is potential future compensation payable to the employee, usually in cash. The amount may be

---

* There are a number of relevant statutes, but perhaps the most important is the Employee Retirement Income Security Act (ERISA) of 1974.

† Recent federal legislation, notably new regulations under Section 409(a) set specific guidelines for how non-qualified compensation and other programs must be designed and implemented. As always, consult your tax, legal and financial advisors.

calculated in any reasonable manner. For simplicity, you may choose a specific number payable at a certain date. Alternatively a formula tied to business results may be used to determine the future amount. In the most sophisticated form, the benefit may be tied to the value of the business as determined by an appraisal. This creates "synthetic" or "phantom" stock as the employee does not have actual ownership, but benefits are tied to the value of the business.

However it's calculated, the potential amount should be large enough to be meaningful to the employee but not excessive or unreasonable. A starting point is the employee's current compensation. An employee earning $250,000 per year may not feel handcuffed for $50,000 per year. Likewise, an owner probably does need to create a $250,000 annual income stream to effectively handcuff a $50,000 salaried employee. Different benefits may be offered to different employees at the same business as long as they are reasonable. Cash benefits once earned are typically paid on an installment basis rather than a lump sum to reduce the owner's cost of funding the benefit. For example, a $1 million potential benefit may be paid to the employee as $100,000 per year over 10 years or even $50,000 per year over twenty years.

Vesting Schedule

A vesting schedule defines how long the employee must remain with the business to earn the potential compensation. Any reasonable approach may be used. Your objective is to tie the employee to the business until at least your likely exit age. Passers and Innies may want to go further and tie the employee to the business until the employee's normal retirement age if it's farther in the future. Vesting may be a cliff, which means vesting occurs all at once, or vesting may occur incrementally over time.

Different employees may receive different schedules. Employees, of course, prefer shorter vesting schedules. There are several ways to fit the interests of both the owner and employee. Avoid a cliff vesting schedule much longer than ten years if possible. Even the most loyal top employee may find it hard to be excited about a benefit that is twenty years in the future. Consider a rolling vesting schedule which breaks the cash benefit into batches earned over several years.

Double Lock Up

Andrew, a Passer, wanted his two children to one day own his successful supply business. Several non-family employees were extremely valuable to the business. Andrew did not want to risk losing them not only while he was the owner, but also after his children took over the business. Andrew wanted these employees to stay with the business until their retirement age, in some cases twenty five years away. If program withheld benefits for as long as twenty-five years it might fail to motivate and retain those employees.

We implemented at Andrew's company a Golden Handcuffs program for these top employee that staggered vesting into five year increments. For example, for one forty-five year old employee the vesting schedule provides that every five years this employee vests in 25% of the total promised compensation. Thus, the employee would not fully vest in the entire program for twenty years, but earn some of the fruits of their labor well before retirement. Andrew effectively locked up the top employees for the rest of his future working years as well as much of his children's working years.

Funding Vehicles

Golden Handcuffs programs do not require setting aside any funds in the present to create the future cash payments; all benefits may be paid from business cash flow. Most owners implement some funding mechanism to be prudent and to demonstrate commitment to the included employees. A commonly used funding vehicle is cash value life insurance. While cash value life insurance typically bears higher expenses than other vehicles, in this situation it offers two advantages. First, life insurance coverage may be already needed for key employee insurance, so the same policy serves a dual purpose. Second, life insurance offers income tax advantages: cash value grows tax deferred, when it is time to pay the promised benefits the policy's cash value may be accessed without income taxes through a combination of withdrawing cost basis and policy loans, and the policy death benefits may reimburse the business for some to all of its cost of creating the golden handcuffs plan.*

---

* Outstanding loans and withdrawals will reduce both the death benefit and cash value.

Legal Agreement

Golden Handcuffs plans and other non-qualified benefits programs should include a legal agreement between the business and the included employee. The agreement explains the plan and helps insure that the plan complies with relevant guidelines. The agreement should specify how the employee earns the future benefits, and what actions would forfeit the benefits.

Playbook: Employment Agreement

Employment agreements are commonly used to address routine issues such as compensation and benefits, but they may also reduce the risk of key employee defection or reduce the damage if that should occur. A competent attorney may recommend up to three different provisions to reduce your risk:

- Non-competition: restricts or prohibits the employee from competing with your business after termination, usually for a defined period (such as one year) and within a defined geographic limitation (such as within 50 miles of your place of business)

- Non-solicitation: restricts or prohibits the employee from attempting to lure away your existing customers or employees should the employee leave and join or become a competitor

- Non-disclosure: restricts or prohibits the employee from revealing or using confidential information about your business, usually for a specific duration after termination.

Your agreement will need to comply with state or local laws and fit your needs. Consult with your legal and other advisors.

Conclusion

The mindset and tactics needed to protect your business and its value are different from the mindset and tactics you use to grow it. This can make it difficult to give enough thought and planning to risk management. Do not allow yourself or your advisors to gloss over risk management in your exit planning. You've worked too hard not to.

Key Points:

- Risk management is an essential part of exit planning because threats that undermine the business jeopardize not only current profitable operations but also the future value you need from your business.

- Buy-sell plans are one of the most important and least well-utilized risk management tools.

- If you have co-owners in your business, compare your answers to the Seven Essential Questions to reduce the risk that the owners have opposing exit agendas.

- Even if you have built a business that successfully runs without you, should something happen to you the business's value may nosedive.

- Consider "golden handcuffs" plans to retain and motivate top employees to grow the business for at least as long as your exit timeframe.

4

Reducing Your Exit Magic Number

In Chapter Two we defined and discussed the Exit Magic Number. It forecasts the value to extract from your business to achieve your financial freedom. Because the number is a reflection of financial dependency on your business to achieve exit goals, generally a lower number is better and the ideal number is zero. If your Exit Magic Number was zero, then you could afford your desired lifestyle without unlocking any of the wealth in your business. Nobody is suggesting you would just walk away from your business, but the financial ability to walk away creates immense flexibility and options in your exit planning. The owner who needs every penny from the business often has the most difficult or expensive (think taxes) path to exit. Remember it's usually easier to exit from a $5 million business with $5 million in the personal bank account than to exit from a $10 million business with $0 in the personal bank account.

The Three T's: Timing, Terms and Taxes

We've said that a lower Exit Magic Number creates more flexibility and control. Control of what? A large part of the answer is the Three T's of your exit: Timing, Terms and Taxes. If you recall, part of the definition of exit planning includes "...efficiently growing and converting your private business ownership..." Efficiently converting the business value into personal wealth is determined by the timing of the conversion, the terms of the conversion and the taxes on the conversion. Specifically, it's the timing and the terms that largely drives the taxes.

For example, assume you sell your business's stock for $10 million in cash. (As always, add or subtract zeros as you see fit to match your situation.) In this example, the timing was "at closing." The terms were all-cash. And the taxes, as we will explore later will be determined by the rules for a stock sale.

Let's change the example. Assume you sell your business for $10 million, but agree to be paid $1 million per year for ten years plus interest. It's still a $10 million sale, but the Three T's have changed. The timing is now spread out over ten years. The terms now include an installment sale plus interest, and the taxes will now be different from the previous example. The combinations and examples are endless.

Here's why this is important. Your ability to influence or even dictate the timing, terms and thus taxes is largely driven by your dependency on the business. If you are highly dependent on the business, exhibited by a high Exit Magic Number, then you're like the consumer who for some reason must buy a car today—you likely will not get the best price, the lowest interest rate on financing or your favorite color. If you made the conscious effort to reduce your dependency by building wealth and sources of income outside your business, then you've positioned yourself to pursue the most favorable timing, terms and taxes.

Perhaps the biggest obstacle to efficiently lowering your Exit Magic Number will be taxes. If taxes were not an issue, then you could simply pay yourself a large salary or bonus each year and invest the cash in some desired way. In the real world, those large bonuses create large income and payroll taxes. This chapter will introduce systematic tactics for your Playbook to convert your business's current cash into wealth outside the business and reduce your Exit Magic Number.

Playbook: Tax-Leveraged Retirement Plans

Many American employees consider their company's retirement plan to be the primary tool to accumulate assets for retirement. Many business owners consider retirement plans to be a big fat headache. Owners have good reasons to be frustrated: time-consuming enrollment and education, incomprehensible investment performance, and high administrative costs. Small to medium size businesses often lack in-house experienced employee benefits professionals, leaving the owner to fend for himself. Perhaps the biggest disappointment occurs if you personally cannot contribute significant funds because the plan failed anti-discrimination tests or because contribution limits are too low for your needs.

Despite this, properly designed retirement plans present a powerful tool to tax efficiently build wealth outside of the business. Qualified retirement plans usually receive special tax incentives such as income tax deductible contributions and tax deferred growth on plan investments. The ability to deduct contributions and defer taxation greatly increases potential net accumulations.

Selecting the Ideal Plan Design

Retirement plans generally must include all eligible employees to comply with anti-discrimination rules. In our experience most owners are not opposed to providing retirement benefits to their employees, but they don't like it when anti-discrimination rules or plan contribution limits restrict their ability to put meaningful dollars into the plan. If this is the case, often it means you are using the wrong type of retirement plan. If your primary objective is to provide a cost-effective benefit to employees, then typically the ideal plan is the universally-recognized 401(k). If your primary objective is to build wealth for you, then the ideal retirement plan commonly will *not* be a standard 401(k). This is where the confusion begins.

Section 401(k) plans have come to dominate the retirement plan marketplace over the last generation. Employees and employers like many of their features. With a 401(k), employees make a personal choice to defer a portion of their paycheck into the plan, reducing their income taxes as they accumulate retirement savings. Employers chose whether or not to match employee deferrals to sweeten the pot. Because of its flexibility in today's transient labor environment, the 401(k) is the preferred plan for the business that seeks to provide a cost-effective retirement employee benefit.

The wide recognition 401(k) plans enjoy causes some owners to assume this plan will meet their own retirement and exit planning needs. Standard 401(k) plans usually are poorly suited to meet your needs; the flexibility that makes the 401(k) attractive is often its undoing for you. Because employees individually chose to participate or not, often it's higher paid employees with more discretionary income that contribute most of the dollars. If lower paid employees contribute little relative to more highly paid employees, then the plan may fail anti-discrimination tests designed to prevent this imbalance. Once this occurs the plan administrator usually reduces your contributions (and contributions from other higher paid employees) to bring the plan into compliance. You may have had this happen to you. It leaves the business owner with the double negative of less money in the plan and higher income taxes. The smaller the number of plan participants other than you, the greater potential this occurs. While we have seen 401(k) plans with several thousand employees experience this problem, companies with several hundred employees or less commonly have the most difficulty complying with the anti-discrimination rules.

Other types of retirement plans may better serve your goal of tax-efficiently building wealth outside the business. To evaluate which plan design may be the best fit, we created two tools: the concept of *Tax Leverage* and the *Target Contribution Ladder*. Tax Leverage exists when potential income tax savings created by the plan exceed the costs of providing the plan.* Plan costs include expenses that the business incurs to maintain and fund the plan including contributions required for rank and file employees plus any plan administrative fees. Consider the hypothetical example in Table 4-1:

Table 4-1: Tax Leveraged Retirement Plan Example

Total retirement plan contributions	$50,000
Owner's portion of the total	$40,000
Rank and file employees' portion of the total	$10,000
Plan administrative costs	$4,000
Total retirement plan costs	$14,000
Potential income tax savings @35% tax rate	$17,500 ($50,000 x .35)
Tax Leverage	$3,500 ($17,500 - $14,000)

Tax Leverage is just a simple analysis to help evaluate if the plan benefits the owner. The greater the Tax Leverage then the more efficiently the retirement plan helps you accumulate wealth outside of your business.

If the goal is to select the retirement plan type that creates the most Tax Leverage, then the question becomes which plan type? To help you and your

---

* Investment costs such as mutual fund expenses or an investment advisor's fees, are excluded from this analysis because typically those costs would be incurred if you invested outside of a retirement plan.

advisors determine this, use the Target Contributions Ladder. This charts the suggested plan types based on the amount you wish to contribute each year for members of a target group such as yourself, family members employed in the business or even top employees. While every business is different, the Target Contributions Ladder identifies which plan may provide you with the maximum tax leverage. To determine your target annual contribution per person, start with your constraints. How much can the business afford to contribute? How large an income tax deduction is desired? Typically you and your advisors can determine the ideal contribution for that year and perhaps even several future years. As your desired target contribution increases, we move up the Target Contribution Ladder and the ideal plan types change.* From there, how many employees you have will help determine the ideal plan for your business.

Table 4-2: Target Contributions Ladder

If the Target Annual Contribution per Person is...	Then Consider These Plan...
More than $50,000	Defined Benefit Plans: Pension, Cash Balance, Combination
About $20,000 to $50,000	Defined Contribution Plans: Solo-K, Profit Sharing, Safe Harbor
About $10,000 to $20,000	SIMPLE IRAs
Up to $10,000	Personal IRAs

A brief description of each option is provided below, starting with the bottom of the ladder and moving up.

Target Contributions Up to About $10,000 per Person

The initial rung on the Target Contribution Ladder is for owners that desire a current contribution up to about $10,000. For this owner the ideal company retirement plan may be none. If you are married and file a joint income tax return with your spouse, you may contribute about $10,000 combined into personal IRAs. If you do not participate in retirement plans at work, contributions to a Traditional IRA usually are income tax deductible

---

* The precise contribution limits for these plans change nearly every year. This book uses general numbers as much as possible to anticipate that the specific amounts change frequently.

depending on income limitations. This provides you with the same potential income tax benefits created by a retirement plan at the business, without the costs and headaches of setting up a plan at the business.

Target Contributions from About $10,000 to $20,000 per Person

If you seek to contribute up to about $20,000 per person, the ideal plan may be the Savings Incentive Matching PLan for Employees (SIMPLE). Under current laws employees may contribute 100% of their earned income up to a maximum of more than $10,000 into a SIMPLE. In addition the business must select a mandatory contribution of either two percent for all eligible employees or match dollar-for-dollar up to the first three percent of wages. If you have wages of $200,000 for example, a three percent match creates an additional $6,000 into your SIMPLE account. Owners age 50 and older are permitted additional "catch up" contributions. With a SIMPLE it's possible to approach about $20,000 in total contributions per person.

SIMPLE plans do not require anti-discrimination tests, so low employee participation does not jeopardize your ability to contribute the maximum. However, high employee participation may reduce or even eliminate Tax Leverage. A company with 50 eligible employees with average compensation of $40,000 has a $2 million payroll. The flat two percent company contribution would cost the owner $40,000 and probably wipe out any Tax Leverage. If the three percent match is used, the actual employee participation and wages will determine the Tax Leverage. Other important SIMPLE IRA provisions include immediate *vesting* for company contributions. Vesting is the period of time an individual must remain with the business and eligible for the plan benefits to keep the business's contributions upon termination. The employees' personal contributions are always immediately vested. Only businesses with 100 eligible employees or less may offer SIMPLE plans. For the business owner with a target contribution amount up to $20,000 per person the SIMPLE may be ideal.

Target Contributions from About $20,000 to $50,000 per Person

What if your target contribution is greater than $20,000 per person, or if your business has more than 100 eligible employees? The next rung on the Target Contribution Ladder features a family of retirement plans known as defined contribution plans. Defined contribution plans limit the maximum contribution, currently more than $45,000 per person per year. Determining which plan to use depends on the size and demographic make-up of your employee group.

Up to About Five Eligible Employees

There are two common options for owners with a few employees, generally up to five. Until recently the only option was a SEP (Simplified Employee Pension) IRA. Under a SEP, your business makes discretionary contributions up to 25% of the eligible payroll. All participants must receive the same contribution percentage. If you are the only employee, then this does not present a problem. However, if the business has additional eligible employees then Tax Leverage dissipates quickly. For example, if an owner has $200,000 in earnings and ten other eligible employees who average $40,000 in income, then the total eligible payroll is $600,000. If this owner contributes $40,000 into the SEP (20% of wages) for himself then he must contribute 20% in for everybody else—another $80,000. The larger the number of eligible employees then the less Tax Leverage a SEP usually creates. Like with SIMPLEs, SEPs do not permit a vesting schedule, so the business's contributions immediately belong to employees.

Several years ago a tax law change created another option for owners with few or no additional employees (other than possibly close family members). The new plan is commonly called a "Solo-K" or other similar names. Solo-K plans have one advantage over SEPs: more dollars may be contributed into a Solo-K than possible with SEP if your earnings are about $200,000 or less. Making the same contribution with lower earnings reduces self-employment taxes. This is possible because Solo-K plans allow employees, including you of course, to contribute dollars into the plan in addition to the business's contributions. Solo-K plans may be particularly effective if your business is an S corporation because you have the option to take dividends from your business without double-taxation in lieu of wages.

With More than About Five Employees

If you desire to contribute between about $20,000 to about $50,000 per year but have more than a handful of employees, a SEP or Solo-K may fail to provide positive Tax Leverage. In these situations a profit sharing plan may be the most effective plan type.* Profit sharing plans permit discretionary company contributions for all eligible employees up to 25% of eligible payroll, with a maximum per person contribution of more than $45,000 under current laws. Once the decision is made to make a profit sharing contribution, how those dollars are allocated among the plan participants creates the opportunity to achieve Tax Leverage. In other words, if your

---

* Profit sharing plans get their name from many years ago when, to be eligible to make a contribution, the business had to show profits. This is no longer required but the name stuck.

business is going to contribute $100,000 into a profit sharing plan, how does it get divided up?

There are several methods for how profit sharing contributions may be allocated among plan participants. The method I encounter most often with existing profit sharing plans, *pro rata* (or *salary ratio*), is usually the least beneficial to the business owner. Briefly pro rata plans allocate the contributions in proportion to each person's compensation. Often this fails to create Tax Leverage because you receive the same proportionate share as your other employees.

While several other allocation methods exist, the method that often maximizes Tax Leverage for owners is called *new comparability.* This method divides employees into specific classes and formulates different benefits for those classes. A valid business reason must exist for the classifications; but in many cases it is possible for the owner or owners to be a class by themselves. Consider the example provided in Table 4-3. In our experience, the new comparability allocation method can tax-efficiently accumulate dollars outside your business and reduce your Exit Magic Number.

Table 4-3: New Comparability Plan Example: Founders Inc.

Employees	Wages	Profit Sharing Plan Contribution
Frank Founder	$225,000	$45,000
Frannie Founder	$100,000	$30,000
20 eligible employees	$600,000	$20,000
10 non-eligible employees	$300,000	$0
Total contributions		$95,000
Owners' contributions		$75,000
Percent for owners		79%

Figures are hypothetical.

Safe Harbor Plans

A plan provision called safe harbor may increase Tax Leverage. Safe harbor plans automatically pass anti-discrimination testing (they "sail into a safe harbor") by making one or more mandatory contributions specified in

---

* When this allocation method was first devised, it was "new." The method is no longer new but the name stuck.

the regulations. Because a safe harbor plan automatically meets the anti-discrimination requirements, you and any other highly compensated employees may contribute the maximum into the plan regardless of how much or little your other employees contribute. The disadvantage of safe harbor plans is they reduce flexibility: contributions are mandatory during that plan year and are immediately vested for the employees.

Target Contributions Greater than $50,000 per Person

This is the top rung of the contribution ladder. If you seek annual contributions this size or larger, consider a set of plans known as defined benefit plans. With defined benefit plans, the law does not limit the individual or business contributions. Rather, the law sets a maximum benefit that a plan may provide to a participant at retirement, currently close to $200,000 per year under current laws. Plan contributions are determined by how much needs to be contributed today to create a pool large enough to pay out the yearly benefit set by the plan. This benefit is often expressed as a percentage of average compensation and years of service. Therefore, employees with higher earnings and longer time of employment may receive the largest benefits. Often you are one of the oldest, most highly paid and longest tenured employees. In this case, a defined benefit plan may create an annual tax deductible contribution as large as several hundred thousand dollars per year.

The most common form of a defined benefit plan is a traditional pension plan. Pension plans once dominated the retirement plans landscape, when employees commonly worked for the one company their whole career. Traditional pension plans have declined in use partially because today's highly transient labor force undermines the need for companies to provide this expensive benefit. However, in your business the cost of providing the benefits may be far less than the income tax savings—thus creating Tax Leverage. Consider the example in Table 4-4:

Table 4-4: Defined Benefit Plan Example: XYZ Law Firm

Employee	Age	Wages	Annual Plan Contribution	% of Total
Partner 1	63	$400,000	$163,169	40.8%
Partner 2	57	$375,000	$148,693	37.2%
Partner 3	35	$225,000	$26,844	6.7%
Partner 4	35	$225,000	$23,269	5.8%

Paralegal 1	51	$65,000	$18,055	4.5%
Paralegal 2	49	$65,000	$14,779	3.7%
Clerk 1	26	$40,000	$2,616	0.7%
Clerk 2	24	$40,000	$2,229	0.6%
Totals		$1,460,000	$399,724	100%

Figures are hypothetical.

Closely-held business owners considering a defined benefit plan must carefully weigh the potential benefits with the plan's inflexibility. Unlike 401(k) and profit sharing plans, defined benefit plans generally require that the contributions be made each year. If your business faces uncertain future cash flow, a defined benefit plan may not be appropriate. To give more flexibility, consider a combination defined contribution/defined benefit plan. Under a combination plan you may reduce or skip the profit sharing contribution in any given year.

Qualified retirement plans are complex and the landscape constantly changes: laws are amended, your employee population evolves and your business condition changes. These changes affect retirement plan design and maintenance. You and your advisors must evaluate at least annually any plan you use. Your effort may bear fruit because these tools permit you to use tax deductible dollars to build wealth outside the business in support of your exit plan.

Playbook: Roth 401(k) Plans

Another type of qualified retirement plan that may be well suited to helping you reduce your Exit Magic Number is the Roth 401(k). These plans were first available to US employers in 2006 and have been growing in popularity since then. They are taxed generally the same way as Roth IRAs—contributions are after-tax, meaning you pay income taxes upfront. From there the assets will grow without being taxed and generally may be withdrawn without income taxes after normal retirement age of 59½. Roth 401(k)s are potentially attractive because most successful business owners have very few opportunities to create income tax free dollars. For example, you may not fund a Roth IRA in any year your adjusted gross income exceeds a certain level—about $160,000 per year if you are married and file a joint tax return. With Roth 401(k) plans there is no such income limitation. Most other 401(k) rules and limitations apply.

Playbook: Asset Lease Backs

Another second systematic tool to reduce your Exit Magic Number is known as an asset lease back. Under this structure you purchase or create assets outside of your business that you turn around and lease back to your business for commercial use. The most common asset for a lease back is the real estate your business uses in its normal operations. Other assets to consider include business equipment and even intangible property such as patents, copyrights or trademarks. Ideally place the asset into a separate legal entity such as an LLC or S corporation to create potential creditor protection and income tax planning flexibility. There are many potential advantages with this tool:

1) Lease payments are generally income tax deductible to your operating business.

2) Income earned from the lease back is usually not subject to payroll taxes.

3) Buildings, equipment and some other items may create income tax savings through depreciation.

4) Appreciation on the market value of the asset is usually income tax deferred until sold.

5) The assets held outside the business usually are not at risk from the business' creditors.

6) When you ultimately exit, you may decide to keep those outside assets and lease them back to the new owners or to another party.

If any debt on the assets exists, paying it down during your working years increases the potential net income available for you after exit.

Playbook: Adopt a M.O.O.S.E.

The tools offered here to reduce your Exit Magic Number have been described as *systematic*, which in this context means they happen **automatically happen once established.** For example, once an asset lease back is set up the lease payments and potential wealth-creation benefits happen each month while you go back to work. The best tools to reduce your Exit Magic Number use a disciplined approach to getting results. Look at your business's strengths and usually you will find effective systems.

M.O.O.S.E. stands for Monthly Out Of Sight Earning. Adopting a M.O.O.S.E. means setting up a regular monthly dollar amount that you set aside each month without the business missing it—operations will not be harmed and growth will not be compromised. Would your business miss $100 per month? Would it miss $500? $50,000? Somewhere above $1 is an amount you would not miss. This is your M.O.O.S.E. Once you have identified the amount, set up a regular monthly contribution through using an automatic sweep from a checking account or instructing your bookkeeper or controller to automatically cut a monthly check. It must be automatic and out of your sight. If you have to remember to do this each month, or if you have to rely on yourself to stay disciplined, your M.O.O.S.E. will never get fed and die a horrible death.

There may or may not be income tax benefits with your M.O.O.S.E. If you have exhausted income tax deductible strategies like a retirement plan, your M.O.O.S.E. may be after-tax dollars. What's important here is not tax savings but systematically building assets outside your business to reduce your Exit Magic Number. How you invest your M.O.O.S.E. is up to you and your advisors. If you are like most successful business owners and have little personal liquidity, consider vehicles that build liquid net worth.

The Forgotten M.O.O.S.E.

Conner had been a client for about four years when he sat down in our offices for an annual review. His business had consistently performed well with over $20 million per year and strong profit margins. As we were discussing his personal financial statement, he pointed to one item showing an account worth about $285,000. Conner looked up and asked, "What is that?"

"That," I replied, "is your M.O.O.S.E."

Four years earlier Conner had reluctantly agreed to set up the M.O.O.S.E. At first he resisted, saying no investment could grow faster than his business so it did not make sense to him to invest outside his business. He only agreed because he had almost no assets outside his business and his home. After some discussion, he had asked his controller Amy if his business could cash flow $5,000 per month. She said yes, so we established an automatic monthly transfer of that amount to an after-tax investment account outside the business.

Conner had been receiving quarterly statements for his M.O.O.S.E. account, but during this review he stopped to pay attention to it for the first time. "That is my M.O.O.S.E.?" he responded. "I remember us talking about it, but I forgot it was there. It's grown to that much?" After discussing the account he looked up from the statement and said, "Double it."

Playbook: Reinvest/Receive Ratio

Another systematic tool for reducing your Exit Magic Number occurs annually rather than monthly. Like the M.O.O.S.E. it's primarily about a disciplined approach to helping increase wealth outside the business as you grow your business. Most businesses go through some budgeting process for each new year. As you are going through your budget process, ask the following: If your business makes a profit this coming year, what percent will the CEO in you *reinvest* back into the business and what percent will the owner in you *receive* and take home? Your answer is your *Reinvest/Receive Ratio*. For example, you may decide that you are going to reinvest 65% and receive 35%. Write the ratio down and the reasons behind your decision. At year end, review the ratio and follow your own advice.

When first introduced to this tool, most owners quickly point out how nobody can predict the future, profits are not guaranteed, owners need to be prudent, etc. I completely agree. Setting up your Reinvest/Receive Ratio a year in advance requires assumptions. Things may not happen as forecasted. The ratio is not set in stone and you may have to override your own decision when you reach the end of the year. Here's why the tool works: if you do not set any guideline, then twelve months later when you have actual cash in your business checking account you risk making an undisciplined decision. Your business will have opportunities and initiatives that could easily absorb 100% of any surplus. Most businesses never run out of ways to spend new money. A Reinvest/Receive Ratio reminds and guides you, in your own words, how to allocate any surplus.

When Will Our Family Come First?

During our first meeting with Mark and his wife Teresa, she sat in our offices and cried. Mark had pumped every dollar he made back into his business since founding it. While they had built an extremely successful business and a large personal net worth, nearly every penny sat inside their business. Teresa felt great anguish because she saw millions in business debt, years of past sacrifices and no game plan for how they could one day achieve financial freedom.

Over the course of our work we identified a number of ways to alleviate their stress including diversifying outside of the business for the first time in their lives. Mark acknowledged they were overdue to build more assets outside the business and offered to take as much out of the business "as he could afford after year end." Teresa strongly objected. "Mark," she said, "that's the way it's always been. That just leaves the issue up in the air until you know that the business is taken care of. When will our family come first?" Mark sat in silence for a few moments, reflecting on his wife's concerns.

"You're right," he said. We discussed defining a Reinvest/Receive Ratio to set clear expectations for the business and their family. Mark set the ratio at 50/50 and has successfully followed the guideline every year since. Both of them are less stressed knowing that they have a tool in place to reduce their dependency on the business until the inevitable exit.

Set the ratio and make every effort to stick with it. Perhaps you had decided to take home 35% but at year end realize that only 25% is feasible. Take the 25% home and consider making 35% the target again for next year. Like with the M.O.O.S.E., consider investing the funds in any vehicle that increases your liquidity and diversifies your assets.

Playbook: Ideal "Strategic" Asset Allocation

The fifth and final tool to reduce your Exit Magic Number while you are growing your business borrows from the investment advisor's toolbox. If you have met with an investment advisor, it probably did not take long before you and the advisor were reviewing various investment graphs and charts, especially pie charts. The investment community appears to love pie charts. One common exercise compares two pie charts side-by-side: the first illustrating how your liquid investments currently are allocated among different asset classes like stocks, bonds, cash etc. and the second illustrating how this current allocation compares to an ideal model given your investment objectives. This exercise quickly identifies where you may have too much of one type of asset and not enough of another, potentially increasing risk and undermining performance. It's a helpful tool for managing liquid portfolios, but the reality is for many successful closely-held business owners the liquid portfolio is only a small slice of the total asset pie. Most of your wealth sits not in liquid assets but in the business and its supporting assets.

A "strategic" asset allocation elevates this exercise and compares side by all of your assets against an ideal strategic allocation rather than just examining your liquid portfolio. For example, assume that 80% of your net worth is tied up in your business, 15% in real estate and 5% in cash. Is that your ideal? If not, what would your ideal strategic asset allocation look like? The tool is particularly effective in identifying any need you have for greater liquidity. Work with your advisors to determine the ideal model. Then make and monitor decisions that attempt to move you closer to that ideal.

Table 4-5: Strategic Asset Allocation Example

Asset Type	Current Allocation	Ideal Allocation
Closely held business	80%	60%
Illiquid real estate	8%	10%
Marketable securities in retirement (illiquid) accounts	4%	10%
Marketable securities in after-tax (liquid) accounts	2%	15%
Cash	6%	5%
Total	100%	100%

Figures are hypothetical.

You may never reach your ideal allocation while you are an owner, especially if your business grows in value faster than your other assets. But you will be making conscious decisions and taking prudent actions to grow and build assets outside the business to reduce your Exit Magic Number. Success using the previous four plays helps achieve your desired strategic asset allocation.

Conclusion

Reducing your Exit Magic Number helps you achieve the most favorable arrangement of the Three T's (Timing, Terms and Taxes), which in turn helps you successfully exit. You and your advisors may come up with other ways to tax-favorably reduce your dependency on your business without harming your ability to grow your business. It all starts with understanding how this benefits you and your commitment to put systematic tools in place.

Key Points:

- Your Exit Magic Number is a statement of financial dependency on your business.

- Reducing your Exit Magic Number reduces risk and helps favorably align the Three T's (Timing, Terms and Taxes) of your exit.

- Some tools offer favorable income tax treatment, which allows you to potentially build wealth faster.

- Systematic tools to reduce your Exit Magic Number— meaning you don't have to remember to do them—are most effective.

- Review the five tools offered here and discuss how they may be implemented in your business.

Where to Go From Here

Each of the next chapters focuses on one of the four different exit strategies. You are welcome to read all four, but if your likely exit strategy is clear then consider reading just the chapter discussing your strategy:

Chapters nine and ten pull all readers back together and wrap things up.

5

The Passer's Game Plan

A Passer's defining motivation is to smoothly transfer the business to a successor family member or members. Paramount importance is placed on keeping the business going forward for the next generation. You're willing to make the effort and even take some risks and sacrifices to make this happen. As long as personal financial security and freedom is achieved, most Passers are not concerned about getting "maximum value" for the business. You act from the heart rather than the wallet.* (In this chapter we will assume that Dad and Mom are passing the business down to a single child unless otherwise stated. The tools and tactics discussed in this chapter generally will apply if you are considering passing the business to a family member who is not your child, or if you have multiple children involved.)

---

* I have met a small number of business owners who have wanted their child to buy the business for full and fair market value no matter how much or little income the parent needed from the business for personal financial freedom. The reasoning is if the child purchases the business then the experience will teach the child to better appreciate the business and avoid any kind of "silver spoon" effect. In that situation, the exit plan would more closely resemble that of an Innie—you intend to sell your business to an insider key employee and the family relationships bear little relevance on this issue. If you feel this may be your situation, consider reading both this chapter and Chapter Seven: The Innie's Game Plan.

Passers face a journey quite different from the other exit strategies. Some questions they alone must face and answer, such as "How do I guarantee my kids don't blow it?" Some potential issues they alone must tackle, such as how to be fair to children not actively working in the family business. Woven into these issues and questions are family dynamics, relationships and realities. Being a family owned and lead business is often simultaneously your greatest challenge and your greatest strength.

The first four chapters provided an exit planning foundation that largely applies to all business owners. This chapter focuses on how Passers can create exit plans that address their unique challenges and play to their inherent strengths. The most important issues Passers may face are covered in this chapter:

1)   Creating Financial Freedom for You

2)   Transferring Control in an Orderly Manner

3)   Transferring Ownership in an Orderly Manner

4)   Treating Fairly All Your Heirs

5)   Insuring Adequate Estate Liquidity

For each of these issues, the chapter presents and discusses plays for the Passer's Playbook that may assist with getting closer to end zone.

Issue One: Creating Financial Freedom for You

Few Passers would turn over to a child the keys to their business if meant undermining or jeopardizing financial security. Putting your financial freedom at risk does no good for you, your child or the business. Achieving financial freedom is not only most owner's primary goal, in this case it's extremely important for Passers. The more financially dependent you are on your business to meet your income needs after you exit, the more difficult passing the business down to your child may be. The business might not be able to afford to pay you what you need without straining cash flow and other financial resources.

Furthermore, payments to Dad and Mom that continue for years and years can strain family relationships. It's understandable that you expect to get paid whatever it takes to meet your income needs. After all, it's your business and would not be here without your sacrifices and efforts. Your child probably acknowledges your expectations, but it's also understandable that at some point your child may ask, "How much is enough?" Otherwise your child runs the risk of paying more for the business than it was worth in the open market. Nobody is wrong or right, but there are conflicting needs.

The first step is to implement every means available to reduce your Exit Magic Number by your target exit age. That is your highest priority. Explain to your child that unless the business puts away the maximum dollars for you today to zero-out your Exit Magic Number, you are going to be looking your child in the eye on payday for many years to come. If your Exit Magic Number is still high after your best efforts to reduce it, you and your family must figure out the most effective means to meet your income needs after exit.

The following tactics—the plays for your Playbook—create tax favorable ways to compensate you up to or after you exit using compensation based methods. In many cases, Passers want to be paid by the business using mechanisms that qualify as compensation because this avoids being taxed twice on the proceeds. Regardless of the type of legal entity your business operates as, compensation, where reasonable, creates an income tax deduction for the business which lowers its cost of making these payments.*

Playbook: Employment Contract

It may be odd to think this way, but you may continue to work at your own business even after your exit. The business may pay you a reasonable amount for your role and responsibilities. The advantages of this tactic are that its simplicity, the business may deduct reasonable compensation and you may keep benefits such as medical insurance, company car, etc. The disadvantages are that your earnings are subject to ordinary income taxes and payroll taxes and you have to do real work or risk the IRS disallowing the tax deductibility.

Clearly establish in the employment contract how many years you will work to manage everybody's expectations. Also, clearly define your roles and responsibilities so that you and your child are not feeling tension or stress surrounding who has control of the business.

---

* Compensation earned by you usually is subject to ordinary income taxes and possibly payroll taxes, which in tandem generally are higher than capital gains taxes. These higher taxes may offset some of the tax deductions created for the business. Like with all tax issues and situations, you must consult your tax advisor and consider your specific situation.

Playbook: Consulting Company

Instead of working as an employee, consider working as a consultant. The business may pay a reasonable amount for your services—often higher than what might be reasonable if you were an employee. The advantages of this tactic include simplicity and more personal flexibility for you as a contractor than is often possible as an employee. The disadvantages are that you cannot access company benefits and earnings would be subject to ordinary income taxes and self-employment payroll taxes. As with the tactic of remaining an employee, establish how many years you intend to be a consultant and define the scope of your services so everybody in the family has clear expectations.

Consider setting up a consulting company to contract for and deliver the services rather than you personally. There are several advantages:

- If you do not immediately need or want the income earned, evaluate a tax deductible retirement plan inside the consulting company to shelter earnings from income taxes.

- Consider setting up your consulting business as a C corporation to provide you with employee benefits such as medical insurance or private long term care insurance in a tax favorable manner.

- If your health deteriorated or if you die prematurely, any unfulfilled services could be delivered by another party hired out by the consulting business. Otherwise unearned revenues could be forfeited.

Playbook: Salary Continuation Plan

A salary continuation plan is a formal compensation plan created by your business to reasonably continue the salary after termination of service for a key employee. Salary continuation plans are often used to honor many years of exemplary service and motivate top employees to stay until normal retirement age. Your business may adopt a salary continuation plan for you as a key employee that begins paying out benefits on our about your exit age.

Salary Continuation Security

Howard, age 59 and his son Derrick, age 30 co-owned a marketing research company they had founded together nearly ten years earlier. Howard was the majority owner and wanted his son to one day have all of the business for little to no cost.

Having started the business later in life, Howard knew he had some catching up to do toward financial freedom. Despite maximum contributions to a profit sharing plan each year and a large M.O.O.S.E. for Howard, his Exit Magic Number remained sizeable.

To address Howard's additional needs, the business established a salary continuation plan that would begin at Howard's retirement and continue for five years. The payments would be based on the average annual salary Howard earned his last three working years. The salary continuation plan helped provide for Howard's financial security, and gave Derrick the personal security of a clearly defined financial commitment after his father's exit.

There are many advantages to this tactic: reasonable payments usually are income tax deductible to the business, you are not required to continue working or consulting and the plan's defined provisions help manage everybody's expectations. Some of the disadvantages include no access to company benefits and your earnings are subject to ordinary income taxes and self-employment payroll taxes.

Another consideration with salary continuation plans is, depending on your accounting practices and tax status, the value of the contingent liability may need to be carried on the business' financial statements. Increasing liabilities without a corresponding increase in assets weakens financial statements. This presents possible challenges in managing the business. Weakening financial statements also potentially lowers the business's value. Because your exit planning may benefit from a reduced business value, Salary Continuation Plans present this somewhat ironic additional advantage.

The plans must be a written document drafted by an experienced attorney, ideally several *years* prior to your exit. Implementing an agreement shortly before your exit undermines your ability to demonstrate the business purpose of the instrument.

Playbook: Lost Wages

Lost wages are payments to an employee to make up for a period of time when that employee received below market compensation. Many owners went through periods when they paid themselves low or even no wages. Comparing these periods against typical compensation for similar positions based on industry, business size and location generates a pool of "lost wages" that may be paid to you now or at exit.

The advantages of lost wages include: reasonable payments are income tax deductible to the business, no requirement to continue working and the specified amount of lost wages helps manage everybody's expectations. Some of the disadvantages include no access to company benefits, earnings are subject to ordinary income taxes and your advisors will need to prepare a compensation study to calculate and validate the lost wages amounts.

Used singularly or in combination with one another, these four tools (Employment Contracts, Consulting Contracts, Salary Continuation Plans and Lost Wages) create post exit income on a tax deductible to the business. Later in the chapter as we look at plays for transferring actual business interests to your child, including tools that also create income for you in the process.

Issue Two: Transferring Control in an Orderly Manner

A second need for many Passers is to achieve an orderly transfer of business control to your child. At some point this requires you letting go. Passers get stuck because they do not how to let go—it's not something you've had to do before. On the contrary, much of your business success probably stems from your ability and willingness to take control up to this point.

This issue is separate and distinct from transferring actual ownership of the business to your child. For many owners, control of the businesses is an incredibly important part of financial, emotional and psychological security. A recent study of several hundred closely-held business owners asked what was important to them about their businesses.* Over 98% identified the "desire to control their own lives" as an important benefit of being a business owner. Consider this against only three percent in the same survey that agreed with the statement "becoming wealthy" was an important motivator. It's easy to see why many Passers equate exit planning with stripping away your biggest, warmest security blanket. The solution is to unbundle control of your business from ownership of your business. This gives flexibility to Passers to accomplish their exit objectives.

---

* *US Small Business Owners: Demographics & Motivations, Financial Advisor, June 2004*

The simplest example of how ownership and control may be separated involves reconfiguring the business into voting and non-voting stock.* Assume your business has 100 shares of stock outstanding, all of which is currently voting stock. Working with your advisors you reconfigure the business into 1 voting share and 99 non-voting shares. Usually this is simple to do and does not trigger any income taxes. From there, assume you give your child all of the non-voting stock but keep the one voting share. What have you done? You gave away nearly all of the *ownership* of the business without reducing your effective control of the business.

That's Not a Happy Exit for Me

When we met Wayne, he was the 72-year old founder and sole shareholder of an industrial cleaning business. His three adult children work in the business and had tried for years to get their father to implement some type of succession plan without success. The children highly motivated to get this done. While they loved their father and respected his authority, they feared the business would not survive their father's death due to high estate taxes, possible disagreement among themselves, or both. Their very jobs and their father's life work were at stake.

Wayne shared that he deeply wanted his children to inherit the company. However, he said he was unwilling to surrender final authority over his business during his lifetime. He leaned across the desk and said, "Why should I give up control when I really don't want to? That's not a happy exit for me."

Wayne's tax and legal advisors recommended recapitalizing his S corporation into one percent voting stock and the balance non-voting stock, and then gifting or selling all of the non-voting stock to his children. Wayne could retain the voting stock until death. Once he understood this tactic, Wayne stopped resisting exit planning and was open to this and many other relevant planning tactics.

---

* This is called recapitalizing the corporation's stock. Issuing voting and non-voting stock is possible for both regular C and subchapter S corporations. S corporations may not have two classes of stock, but the use of voting and non-voting shares does not constitute separate classes. If your business is an LLC, there are no shares of stock. However your LLC operating agreement can establish voting and non-voting units.

Separating ownership and control opens the door to tactics that address these two issues differently in order to best accomplish your exit objectives.

Playbook: Family Development Budget

Your business probably has a budget for strengthening sales, developing new products and services, improving operations and training employees. Presumably you budgeted for these items because they are important for your business and warrant adequate resources. Do you have a budget for developing your family? Most Passers do not. Is your family's development any less important to your business than these other items?

Setting the budget notifies everybody that you take this issue seriously and puts resources into your efforts. A Family Development Budget should be large enough to be significant without being unaffordable. Review your existing financial statements and compare how much you spend to develop other areas of your business. With a budget in hand, investigate resources to help your family development such as workshops, books, family business organizations or outside consultants. The budget, if wisely spent, can provide an immeasurably high return on your investment.

Playbook: Control Checkpoints

Many Passers initially believe that they have to give up control on everything all at once. That is not the case. You and your child benefit from a carefully charted approach where control is gradually and appropriately transferred. Devise a series of Control Checkpoints that plot the path. Assign one set of responsibilities to your child, evaluate progress and turn over more only when the Checkpoints are fully met. Consider the following:

- Diagram with your child the business's organizational chart as it exists today and as it should exist going forward. Discuss your roles today and in the future.

- Together with child, write job descriptions and performance expectations. Identify responsibilities that you have today and prioritize which you intend to delegate and under what circumstances. Define how transfer of control is affected if performance falls short of those expectations.

- Discuss with your child his strengths and weaknesses. Identify a development plan for building on strengths and improving weaknesses.

- Write down the Control Checkpoints and meet monthly to measure progress and address areas that need further attention.

Playbook: Family Business Council

One of the biggest challenges with a family-managed business is clear communications. Maintaining healthy communications is difficult in any business. Add family dynamics into the mix and it only gets harder. A Family Business Council (FBC) creates a structured, scheduled forum for the family to meet and discuss business matters. The Council can help build trust and rapport for both generations, reveal where one or both generations have work to do, avoid potential miscommunications and assist in the younger generation's development as business leaders. Suggested practices to conduct an effective FBC include:

- Meet three to six times per year according to a published schedule.

- Formulate by-laws that lay down how your FBC will operate

- Invite relevant family members, both those actively working in the business and those outside the business but impacted by its performance.

- Share the work: divide responsibility for scheduling, circulating an agenda, keeping minutes, etc.

- Bring in a professional meeting facilitator if you need help getting started, especially if the family recently has experienced discord or divisiveness.

- Invite members of your exit planning team or other advisors to attend part of the meetings to get to know the family and review some of their work for you.

- Rotate responsibility for making presentations or leading discussions. Agenda items can include review financial statements, discussing strategic plans, writing vision or mission statements or any business matter you see fit to discuss.

A Council, a Plan and a Wink

Lucy and her son Matt had been working side-by-side for nearly twelve years. They both wanted Matt to lead the business into a second generation, but Lucy had private concerns. Meeting alone with us, she expressed uncertainty over a "new business expansion plan" Matt had been working on but Lucy had never seen. Lucy was confident in her son, but she felt in the dark about his plans. She told us that even though her office and Matt's were right down the hall from each other, they rarely had any quality time to talk about the business's future. We recommended the family establish a Family Business Council with Lucy, Matt and two additional family members.

We joined them for their first meeting. The agenda was to establish how they wanted their Council to operate and to hear Matt's plan for expanding the business. Matt worked for nearly six weeks on his business plan to get it ready. He pulled in the accountant for help with the numbers and solidified his market research. At the meeting, Matt presented the plan and a three hour discussion followed about the direction of the family business.

At the end of the meeting, Lucy told Matt his plan was exciting and offered some helpful thoughts. She asked for a status report at the next Council meeting. As Lucy stood up from the table, she turned, looked at us and winked. She no longer felt in the dark.

Transferring your control of the business to a successor child is not easy in most situations. Give yourself and your child plenty of time—rushing this process rarely makes it go smoother. The tactics presented here can help your child develop which in turn help you grow more comfortable with letting go when appropriate. If you struggle further with this issue consult your advisors. Family business experts, professional coaches and other resources may help you beyond the tools offered here.

Issue Three: Transferring Ownership in an Orderly Manner

In addition to addressing the transfer of business control, Passers must transfer the actual business ownership in an orderly manner. A closely-held business is an asset, and there are only two ways to transfer ownership of an asset—either sell it or give it away. For Passers, transferring some to all of the business via gift is commonly more desirable. Gifts, when done properly, can be easy, simple and tax-free.

Some owners do not like the idea of gifting business ownership. You worked too hard to create it and now somebody is suggesting that you just give it away? You may also be concerned that giving the business to your child undermines his appreciation for the business and the value of a dollar. A client once made the point clear to me. While on vacation in the southern half of the world, he received an email from us regarding a large gift of his business's stock to his son. From his phone he replied with the following message:

> "I am reading your message in Melbourne, Australia. I don't know if it is being upside down or talking of giving stuff away that is making me feel sick."

These feelings are understandable. Gifting business ownership is not about giving your child something for nothing, or diminishing the value of what you have built. Gifting tactics help accomplish your exit goal of preserving the business for your next generation with minimum cost and taxes. Transferring business ownership via gift usually avoids triggering income or capital gains taxes. However, gifts can potentially trigger transfer taxes, commonly known as gift and estate taxes.

A Short Introduction to Gift and Estate Taxes

Just like income creates the potential for income taxes, gifts potentially trigger gift taxes. If the party making the gift is alive, gift tax rules apply. If the party making the gift is deceased, estate tax rules apply. Until several years ago, the rules for federal gift taxes and estate taxes were largely identical. For this reason the gift and estate tax system was often referred to as the "unified" tax. Tax changes created important differences between gift taxes and estate taxes that require clearly distinguishing between the two.[*]

Gift taxes are the responsibility of the party making the gift, commonly called the grantor. If a business owner gives some or all of the business to a child, any gift taxes are paid by the *owner* and not the child. Many people are surprised to learn this, for it may seem backwards compared to income taxes. Similarly, if a business owner dies and leaves the business to a child, the owner's estate must pay any estate taxes. These taxes usually must be promptly paid: gift taxes are generally due by April 15 following the year of

---

[*] Most notably was the Economic Growth and Tax Reconciliation Recovery Act of 2001 (EGTRRA).

the gift, and estate taxes due generally must be paid within nine months from the date of death. Gift and estate taxes generally use the same tax schedule. Like with income taxes, the tax rate increases as the amount of the assets increases and under current laws can reach 45% of the value of the assets.

Gift and estate taxes present special problems for Passers. Part of the problem is philosophical. Many owners despise the thought that their wealth could be eroded by nearly half its value by a "death tax." They have sacrificed too much: working without pay during lean times, putting personal assets on the line to guarantee business debts, taken risks where others would not. The idea that their business could be cut nearly in half when they try to give it to their children is deeply unsettling.* It's understandable if you don't like the system, but don't let that prevent you from using the available tools to protect yourself and your business.

The tax code offers several methods to transfer assets without triggering gift or estate taxes. Understanding how these four exemptions work will help you evaluate the various tactics to transfer ownership in the most efficient manner:†

1. The Unlimited Marital Deduction

Asset transfers between spouses generally are not subject to transfer taxes, whether alive or through the estate. For example, a deceased husband leaving his entire estate to his wife creates no transfer tax.‡

2. The Annual Exclusion

Asset transfers of a minimal value are not subject to transfer taxes because Congress and the IRS do not want to bother taxing the small stuff. For many years the cutoff was $10,000 per person per year. Recently it has been indexed for inflation and currently is about $12,000. Married couples may combine their annual exclusions to double the amount.

---

* We assume in this chapter that you are giving your business to a child. If your successor heir is a grandchild, additional taxes known as Generation Skipping Transfer Taxes may apply. Consult with your advisors.

† Many states impose taxes on assets transfers as well. Business owners should consult their local estate planning attorneys.

‡ The Unlimited Marital Deduction may not apply if either spouse is not a US citizen.

3. "Asset Transfer Allowance"

US citizens receive tax credits that allow them to transfer up to $3.5 million (as of 2009) of assets to any party without incurring out-of-pocket gift or estate taxes. Married couples may combine to shelter $7 million from transfer taxes. Estate lawyers, accountants and other professionals use a variety of technical terms for this provision such as the *lifetime credit shelter equivalent*. An easier to understand term is the "Asset Transfer Allowance" because this amount represents a pool of assets you are allowed to transfer without incurring taxes. Out of the $3.5 million per person limit, no more than $1 million may be transferred while you are alive. This is a clue that using the $1 million living portion of the Asset Transfer Allowance may be a tax-savings strategy — anything the tax code limits is usually desirable to do.

4. Charitable Gifts

Unlimited transfers to valid charitable organizations are permitted without incurring estate or gift taxes. Charitable gifts may be an important part of some Passer's exit planning as we will discuss.

The Importance of Gifting Now

These four exemptions create opportunities to transfer ownership to your child without triggering gift or estate taxes. Too often these exemptions are misused or unused. In most cases, *Passers should consider gifting business ownership to your child now if you believe the business may appreciate in value.* The longer Dad and Mom wait to transfer ownership of a growing business to the child, the potentially higher the federal transfer taxes (gift or estate taxes) may be. Gifting at least some business ownership now (especially non-controlling ownership — remember we have separated ownership and control) removes from your taxable estate not only the present value of that ownership, but also all potential future growth on that ownership interest. As a result, a greater value is passed to your child with less potential taxes. Care is required however. Make sure your child is committed and capable of this responsibility.

Let's examine how this works. Assume we have two married couples, the Smiths and the Browns, both of whom intend to pass their family businesses down to a child. If we assume both businesses grow at a compound rate of 7.2% per year their value will double in ten years.* The

---

* This is known as the Rule of 72. If you take an interest rate and divide it into 72, the answer will be how many years until the asset doubles in value. An asset growing at a compound annual

Smiths combine their $1 million each Lifetime Asset Transfer Allowance to give now to their child a $2 million interest in their business. The Browns wait ten years and then make the same $2 million gift of their business. Compare the results:

Table 5-1: Gift Now or Later?

	Smith Family	Jones Family
Value of asset today	$2 million	$2 million
Amount gifted today	$2 million	$0
Value at 10 years	$4 million	$4 million
Amount gifted at 10 years	$0	$2 million
Remaining amount still exposed to Dad & Mom's transfer taxes	$0	$2 million
Potential transfer taxes @ 45% rate	$0	$900,000

Figures are hypothetical.

Gifting now leverages the impact in your favor—you shelter from transfer taxes not only the present value but all potential future growth on that asset. With this understanding, let's consider some plays for your Playbook on how to orderly transfer business ownership.

Playbook: Devalue the Business then Give it Away

OK, we are ready to identify ways to transfer ownership to our child. Part one is to *devalue* the business. In most situations, Passers benefit from owning a business with a fair market value as low as is reasonably possible. Not only is this counterintuitive at first, it is also contrary to the conventional wisdom that emphasizes grow your business value as high as possible. Devaluing the business does not mean undermining the business's profitable activities. The goal is to reduce value that may be claimed on a tax return. A lower value creates the potential for lower transfer taxes.

To help understand how devaluing a business works, imagine a husband suggests to his wife that they sell the master bedroom of their family home. (Why would anybody want to do this is a good question. Just play along for

---

rate of 7.2% doubles in value after 10 years. (72 ÷ 7.2 = 10). The Rule of 72 assumes a hypothetical rate of return to illustrate the concept of how interest rates of return can work for you. There are no guarantees that any investment will sustain the same return year after year, and thus no guarantee the value will double in a stated period of time.

a moment.) The couple believes their house is worth $500,000. The total square footage is 4,000 square feet, of which the master bedroom is about 20%. So the husband suggests they list the master bedroom for $100,000 (20% of the home's total value). A sign saying *"Master Bedroom for Sale - $100,000"* is put in the front yard, and the couple eagerly waits for buyers.

Of course, not many buyers are likely to show up. No ready market exists for a master bedroom. Why not? Without owning the entire house, one room offers little benefit. Twenty percent of a $500,000 home is not worth $100,000 to most people. The master bedroom is not worthless. If the couple were determined to sell and kept reducing the price, eventually it will sell — at $1 somebody likely will take the chance. But, it is arguably worth far less than $100,000.

This silly example explains two common methods and rationale for reducing the value of a closely-held business for transfer purposes. The first is called a *discount for lack of control*. Consider the futility of paying $100,000 for a master bedroom. Owning the master bedroom alone would provide little of the benefits of owning a home, because the master bedroom owner would not be able to control the overall use and enjoyment of the home. Similarly, the owner of a minority interest is usually unable to control the company. The second rationale is for devaluing the asset is a *discount for lack of marketability*. Selling partial ownership in a home is a difficult proposition at any price. There's no ready market. Likewise the seller of a minority interest in a closely-held business would likely encounter few potential buyers willing to pay full price.

The logic of these discounts, lack of control and lack of marketability, is generally accepted by the business valuation community and federal tax courts. Discounting your business value potentially lowers the potential gift or estate taxes, increasing the amount of business interest you may gift to your child without taxes.

The discount amount is determined by valuation experts who refer to detailed studies, relevant court precedents and the specific facts of a situation. While recent court cases have produced a combined discount often in the 25% to 35% range, ultimately you must consult your advisors. You must use a professional business appraiser with expertise in this field. The appraiser also should be available to defend the analysis against IRS or court scrutiny should it occur.

From $500,000 Potential Tax to Zero

Trish was ready to fully retire and wanted to immediately give her successful wholesale food supply business to her daughter. However, her advisors estimated that the business's value was too high to give it away without triggering as much as $500,000 in gift taxes.

As an alternative, Trish's attorney recapitalized the business into 1% voting and 99% non-voting shares. The business was appraised, and the appraiser discounted the value of the non-voting shares by about 35% because of lack of control and lack of market. Based on the discounted value, Trish gave her daughter all of the non-voting stock with zero gift taxes. She later sold the 1% voting shares to her daughter under a separate agreement.

Once you have applied all reasonable discounts, give as much as possible (especially a non-controlling interest) to your child.* Remember any portion of the business gifted to your child today removes from your tax exposure not only the present value but all potential future growth as well. Time multiplies the power of gifting, which is why the earlier you get started the better.

There are many ways to gift business interests without triggering taxes. Using the annual exclusion, currently $13,000 per recipient per year per person, a married owner with three children may gift $78,000 of business interest to his children each year without taxes.† If these three children have families of their own, the owner and spouse may gift $156,000 per year by including three other family members such as sons and daughters in law or grandchildren. Remember, time accelerates the benefits of making gifts; not only is the present value of the asset but all future growth on that asset is transferred. Assuming you gifted $156,000 of business stock each year for ten

---

* Consult with your advisors about giving the business interest directly to your child or to a trust set up for your child. There are various pro's and con's to consider.

† A common question regarding spouses using the annual exclusion is what if one of the spouses does not have ownership of the asset intended to gift. For example, can a husband and wife gift stock in the family business using both annual exclusions if only one spouse actually owns the stock? Yes, regardless of which spouse owns the asset to be gifted they may combine their annual exclusion in what is known as gift splitting. When gift splitting is used, a gift tax return (Form 709) must be filed.

years, using a five percent growth rate these annual gifts would add up to nearly $3 million transferred without gift taxes. Whether your closely-held business is large or small, any amount transferred without taxes is helpful. The annual exclusion exemption has one obvious drawback—it is limited to a relatively modest amount per year. For a Passer seeking to transfer a business worth many millions the annual exclusion alone may not be sufficient.

You Must Live to 112

Claude was about 60 years old when we first met him, and wanted this son to have their business. For several years Claude had used his annual exclusion to give his son nine shares of company stock each year based on their accountant's estimated value of the business. However, Claude still owned more than 450 shares. At that rate Claude would need to live past age 112 in order to completely pass the business to his son using only the annual exclusion, assuming no change in the business's value.

When did this math for Claude he said, "Oops. You're right. I thought we were doing it right." Claude's annual gifts were helping, but these alone were not going to get the job done.

If you believe your business has the potential to grow in value—and that's why you and your child are working so hard—then the sooner you gift ownership (at least non-controlling ownership) to your child potentially the better.* To make larger gifts, consider the $1 million ($2 million if you are married) living portion of your Asset Transfer Allowance. Discounting the business and using the Asset Transfer Allowance makes it possible to pass all or nearly all of a business worth several million dollars without gift taxes. However, if your business after discounts is not worth millions but tens of millions, then we've only made a small dent up to this point. Your business may be too large to transfer all or nearly all of the ownership using straight up gifts. If the job is bigger we need look deeper into the Playbook.

---

* Conversely, if you have doubts about the business's growth or feel it may decline in the near future, consider delaying any ownership gifts. Gifting a depreciating asset wastes your gifting allowances.

Playbook: Parallel Business

If your business is too big to give away, another tool that you may consider is to establish a Parallel Business. This involves setting up a new business entity, owned mostly or entirely by your child, alongside your existing business. Move business activities from your existing business to the new business over time. The objective is to shrink the value of your existing business and build value in the new business owned by your child. (If you are not ready to transfer control, initially keep for yourself a small controlling interest in the Parallel Business.) You end up shifting business value without incurring gift taxes as your child's business grows while yours stays flat or declines.

Note that this tool has its disadvantages. First, it will likely require many years to implement. You probably cannot move customers, operations, employees and capital with the flip of a switch. The new business also must stand on its own feet and not be merely a front for your existing business. Outside parties such as bankers, customers and suppliers may need to be consulted to avoid causing harm to essential business operations. Things may get cumbersome with issues such as transferring existing employees to the new business or signing long term contracts with customers and suppliers. Operating two businesses increases overhead costs and administrative workload. Careful planning with your exit planning team is required.

Moving Dirt and Value

Cliff owned a large grading company that he wanted to pass the business down to his son. His problem was the business's appraised value was nearly $50 million because of the all the earth-moving heavy equipment it owned, making the business too large to give away. The exit planning team established a second business entity owned 99% by Cliff's son and 1% by Cliff. The second business entity was not going to conduct grading operations but rather it would purchase and own all new heavy earth-moving equipment going forward. Because their equipment was typically replaced after five to seven years, by the end of that period tens of millions of assets had been shifted into the equipment business owned mostly by Cliff's son.

Consider plays from the Playbook in combinations. For example, gift part of the business to your child and at the same time set up a Parallel Business to shift some of the remaining operations, assets or customers. Few of these tools are mutually exclusive.

The next two plays assist orderly transfers of ownership, but they simultaneously create income for you. We established at the beginning of this chapter that most Passers think with their hearts and not their wallets. If you have a need for additional income to achieve your financial freedom, the following plays may serve a double benefit.

Playbook: Grantor Retained Annuity Trust (GRAT)

Grantor Retained Annuity Trusts (GRATs) are a powerful tool to transfer business ownership to your child at a greatly reduced tax value and simultaneously providing income back to you. GRATs have been in use for a long time and in right circumstances can be highly advantageous.

Despite their exotic name, GRATs are simple in concept. You gift some or all of your business to an irrevocable trust.[*] But, you retain the right to a specified income stream paid back to you for a defined period of time. The income stream comes from the business's earnings. Thus the name: "grantor (you—the person making the grant) retained annuity (the fixed income payment) trust."[†] At the end of the specified time period the business passes down to the trust beneficiary, presumably your successor child.

The major advantage of a GRAT is it transfers the business to your child at a reduced value, reducing potential gift or estate taxes. The business's value is reduced by the value income stream owed back to you. In an oversimplified example, if the business is appraised at $10 million and the present value of the retained income stream is $4 million, then the tax value

---

[*] The term "irrevocable" has a significant meaning here. Once established, an irrevocable is largely fixed in terms of its provisions—changes are generally difficult or outright impossible. This inflexibility is tolerated because of what an irrevocable trust offers—assets transferred to the trust are removed from your taxable estate if proper procedures are followed.

[†] A variation is a GRUT, which is a grantor retained unitrust. In a GRUT, the payments to grantor are not fixed like in a GRAT but rather are a percentage of the trust's assets. This creates flexibility to change payments as the trust assets, presumably the business, change in value over time. However, to administer the GRUT the trust assets must be revalued each year, which would mean reappraising the business each year. In most situations this would be needlessly complicated and expensive.

of the gifted business is only $6 million. Generally the business's gift value is reduced in the following manner:*

- Larger payments back to you lower the value of the gifted business interest

- Longer time periods for the payments to last lowers the value of the gifted business interest

- Lower interest rates on the payments, set by the IRS, lower the value of the gifted business interest.

To further lower the value of the business, use discounting techniques gifting the business to the GRAT. As with any gift, not only is the present value of the business removed from your taxable estate but all future growth as well. The more your business appreciates in value during the GRAT period, the greater the amount you ultimately transfer to your child.

GRATs are quite flexible. Your advisors can model the GRAT in a variety of ways to balance your financial needs with the business's ability to make the payments. If you want to keep control over the business you could gift into the GRAT non-voting stock. You could use multiple GRATs, staggering the business gift, income periods or any other desired result.

There is always a catch, of course. If you (the grantor) should die before the end of the specified income period, the entire value of the business is included in your taxable estate as if the GRAT never occurred. For this reason, care must be taken when setting up the GRAT. The longer the income stream, then the greater the risk that you die before income period is over. Maintain adequate life insurance during the GRAT income period to protect against this risk. Also, consider splitting the business into multiple tiered GRATs such as having a five, ten and fifteen year GRAT. This reduces the amount left in your estate if you pass away before the longest income stream period is over. Another disadvantage with GRATs is the payments to you are not income tax deductible to the business. Despite these limitations, GRATs are a powerful tool that can be used to transfer the business ownership and create post exit income.

---

* It is possible to have the value of the gift even be zero, which is called a "zeroed-out GRAT."

Playbook: Intentionally Defective Grantor Trust (IDGT)[*]

An IDGT is in many ways similar to a GRAT. Your legal advisors set up an irrevocable trust. Like a GRAT, the business interest transferred to the IDGT is removed from your taxable estate so it will pass to your child without transfer taxes. Unlike the GRAT, you sell rather than gift the business interest to the trust. Because the transaction is a sale, gift limitations such as the Asset Transfer Allowance do not apply allowing the IDGT to help transfer larger business interests than possible with a GRAT.

Commonly under an IDGT the Passer sells some or all of the business to the trust in exchange for an installment note paying interest. To make things easy, the IRS sets the interest each monthly, known as the applicable federal rate (AFR). A transfer-tax free shift of ownership from you to your child happens as the business value you sell out of your estate exceeds the value contained in the installment payments coming back to your estate. And like with a GRAT, all future growth of the business interest sold to the trust now occurs outside of your taxable estate.

This trust has a twist. It is "intentionally defective" for income tax purposes, which means any income the trust earns (from the business inside trust) will be reported to you for income tax purposes. In other words, you are taxed on all of the trust's income from the business as if the trust did not exist. Usually any talk of paying taxes is not desirable, but in this case it may be. Somebody is going to have to pay income taxes on the business profits. If you are paying them rather than your business or your child, in essence you are making a tax free gift to the trust. Assume your business inside the trust generated $300,000 of taxable income that year. At an assumed income tax rate of 35% the tax bill is $105,000. If you pay the income taxes, the effect is no different than if you gave $105,000 to the trust and it turned around and wrote the check to the IRS. But in most cases you would not be able to gift $105,000 to the trust without paying gift taxes because it's too large an amount. Paying the income taxes yourself accelerates the value you can pass to the trust and thus to your child without transfer taxes.

IDGTs create another income tax benefit. You are both the seller and, for income tax purposes only, the buyer of the business. Therefore no gain is recognized on the sale in most circumstances. The note payments from the trust back to you usually are income tax free because they are payments back to yourself.[†]

---

[*] As these tools get more powerful, you will notice their names grow more unusual.

[†] See IRS Revenue Ruling 85-13.

There are many details to consider with your advisors before implementing an IDGT. The trust document must be carefully drafted with respect to a number of tax code sections. The debt back to you (the installment notes) must be bona fide and there are requirements on the debt/equity ratio in the trust. Most advisors recommend "seeding" the trust with a gift of at least 10% of the trust's eventual value to meet this ratio. If you and your spouse gift to IDGT your combined lifetime Asset Transfer Allowance of $2 million, that suggests the total sale to the IDGT cannot exceed $18 million. It's possible that an income tax gain may be triggered if you die before the last note payment, so this risk needs to be addressed. Like with any powerful tool, it must be used carefully and properly.

Issue Four: Treating Fairly All Your Heirs

The fourth issue many Passers face is how to be fair to all heirs. (If you have only one child or other heir consider skipping this section.) If you have more than one heir (we will assume it's your children) then your peace of mind may require balance how you pass the business to some heirs yet be fair to the others. The more concentrated your wealth inside your closely-held business, the more difficult things can get.

Every owner that I have worked with wanted to treat all his children "fairly." What does "fair" mean? Fair probably does not mean equal and equal probably does not mean fair in these situations.

The Good Question

Joe was pressured into meeting us by his son. Joe had started his industrial supply business nearly forty years before we met him. While his son had been running the business for the last ten years, Joe still owned all the stock. The son worried how the business would continue at Joe's death without sound planning. Joe welcomed us to his home one morning. Pretty quickly he told us that he did not enjoy discussing this topic.

We asked Joseph what his goals were for his business. He crossed his arms on his chest and replied, "I don't know why this is so hard for everybody. I want my son to get the business and my other kids to be treated fairly. Is that so hard?"

I replied, "OK, I got it. That is clear. But could you tell me, what does 'fair' mean to you?"

Joseph said nothing for about ten seconds. He uncrossed his arms, leaned forward and said with a grin, "Well, that's a good question, isn't it?"

We spent the next two hours chewing on what fair meant to him. Joe opened up and from that point on actually enjoyed designing and implementing his exit plan.

Start with resolving what "fair" means to you. People who do not own a closely-held business often define "fair" as splitting up their assets into equal proportions to be shared with each heir. This straightforward approach rarely works for a Passer. Typically your business is the largest part of your net worth. Splitting up a business among children working in the business and those who don't can create more problems than it solves. Another problem is the tax code encourages Passers to transfer the business now to minimize future potential gift or estate taxes. Transferring some or all of the business to one child now, but not distributing the rest of your assets to other children until much later at your death, can also cause family tension. Finally, how is the value of the closely-held business calculated when determining "fair"? Do you use its fair market value—if so who determines this? How do you take into account any valuation discounts on the business value applied to reduce transfer taxes?

A last reason why the "add-it-up-and-divvy-it-out" approach usually does not work for a Passer is a closely-held business has different characteristics from other assets such as marketable securities or real estate. It is vulnerable to a different set of risks, places different demands on the owners and creates different opportunities.

Not All Assets are Equal (Part One)

Fred and Ginger owned a large food service business and had two children. Their son had worked in the business for nearly twenty years and they wanted to pass the business down to him. Their other child was a daughter who had chosen not to work in the business. When we first met Fred and Ginger, with tears in their eyes they told us how important it was to protect the business for the son but also share their life's blessings with their daughter. Their $10 million net worth largely consisted of only two assets: a business appraised at $5 million and about several hundred acres of raw land also worth about $5 million.

The obvious suggestion was to pass the business to their son and the land to their daughter. The estimated value of both assets was coincidentally equal. However, they saw this action as completely unfair. The business generated significant income each year while the land only generated a sizeable property tax bill. They knew their daughter would not sell the land for sentimental reasons, which meant she would never see the financial rewards that the business could provide her brother. Passing a business to one child and land to another of equal value was not fair to them.

Consider the following ideas and guidelines to help:

- Rather than consider what assets to transfer, identify what *benefits and opportunities* do you want to provide to each child? Transferring a business with an estimated market value of $10 million provides different opportunities (and responsibilities) than $10 million of marketable securities.

- Avoid if possible splitting up the business among heirs who are actively involved and those who are not. Too often it creates family tension and resentment even inside the most caring families.

- Separate income produced by the business from control and ownership of the business. A portion of the business's income may be used to fund strategies that create benefits for children not actively involved in the business. Children that are not actively involved in the business do not need to become owners in order to receive benefits from the business.

Playbook: Family Balancer Trust

If the business is your largest and most valuable asset, create assets for children outside the business to meet your definition of "fair." One tool is the Family Balancer Trust, which establishes a dedicated pool of assets for children who do not receive business interests. You may contribute any asset to the trust, but in many cases the most effective tool is life insurance on you (or you and your spouse). Life insurance creates income and estate tax cash at your death to balance out your estate. Even more helpful, the business may pay for the life insurance, which effectively uses the business to ultimately benefit all of your heirs.

Not All Assets are Equal (Part Two)

The solution for Fred and Ginger believed was a Family Balancer Trust. Fred and Ginger's advisors set up an irrevocable trust which purchased a $1 million life insurance policy payable after they both died. The daughter was the only beneficiary of the trust. Their son would receive the family business and their daughter would receive the raw land plus the tax free cash. This solution felt fair to them and their children.

Playbook: Asset Lease Backs to Inactive Children

If you recall, one of the tactics to reduce your Exit Magic Number is to purchase and lease back to your business assets it uses to operate. Commonly used assets include the real estate the business occupies, the equipment and sometimes even patents and other intellectual property assets. This tactic may help treat all your heirs fairly too. Consider giving (now or at your death) children not active in the business those leased-back assets. This creates a potential income stream from the business for those heirs but without sharing actual ownership.

Playbook: Non-Voting Stock for Inactive Children

Passers should make every effort to treat their heirs equally without actually dividing the business. It creates too much potential for disagreement and discord. Your child working in the business may resent sharing profits with siblings not working in the business. Children not active in the business may resent owning an illiquid asset where profits are held down to reduce income tax taxes. If you must consider dividing ownership among active and inactive children, consider transferring non-voting stock to inactive children. Children not working in the business will not have input on how the business is run, but may enjoy some of the economic rewards such as annual distributions or cash if the business is sold. A buy-sell plan is necessary in these situations.

Issue Five: Insuring Adequate Estate Liquidity

The fifth and final issue that commonly challenges Passers' efforts to successfully exit is adequate liquidity in your estate. Many owners have 75 to 90% or more of their net worth tied up in the business and its supporting assets. Add into the picture real estate and retirement accounts and your net worth may be almost entirely illiquid. Throw on top of this any business or personal debt and insufficient estate liquidity can ruin the best exit plan.

The Cost of Illiquidity

Several years ago Carl, the widower father of a father-son business, passed away only two weeks after hiring us to create his exit plan. Carl's estate included 75% of a business with $30 million in gross sales, about $5 million in other real estate (mostly raw land) and about $300,000 in bank certificates of deposit. With no time to prepare, what happened next was sadly predictable.

The family had to sell nearly all of the land at fire-sale prices to raise cash in a short time. The business suffered because not only did it lose Carl, but Carl's son Ray was spending valuable hours each week dealing with his father's estate. Eventually about half of the nearly one hundred employees were terminated. Competitors began to talk, and for several months rumors circulated that the company was going under.

Only after several years did the business begin to recover, but at the cost of years of stress and millions lost to taxes and assets sold for bargain prices. If Carl had left his heirs with $5 million in cash rather than $5 million in raw land, writing the estate tax check would have been regrettable but easy. No jobs would have been lost, no customers would have left and no stress imposed on the family.

Playbook: Irrevocable Life Insurance Trust

If your estate is not yet large enough to be subject to estate taxes, your hard work growing the business may bring you that dubious reward. As a general rule, avoid owning life insurance inside your taxable estate or even inside your business. If this happens, death benefits may only inflate the size of your taxable estate and add to the tax bill. Life insurance death benefits are usually income tax free but could be subject to estate taxes depending on who or what owned the policy when the insured person dies. A $2 million insurance policy may end up netting only slightly more than $1 million if the entire amount is subject to estate taxes.

A simple solution is to own your life insurance in an irrevocable trust. When probably structured, assets held by and with death benefits payable to an irrevocable trust may be outside your taxable estate. The same $2 million policy now provides $2 million of cash when it's needed rather than just over $1 million. There are a number of important considerations to discuss with your advisors, but in many cases this simple tool does an effective job of protecting your insurance benefits from adverse estate taxation.

Many of the other tactics covered earlier in this chapter and in previous chapters will help reduce your vulnerability to estate illiquidity. Reducing your Exit Magic Number often increases liquidity as you create wealth outside the business. Buy-sell plans address liquidity needs should you die while still an owner. Transferring ownership of your business to your child now potentially reduces your taxable estate in the future. A comprehensive discussion of estate planning is beyond this book, and your advisors may present additional ideas beyond the exit planning focus.

Conclusion

Preserving a business for the following generation can be your greatest accomplishment as an owner. The family business becomes a legacy of your work and achievements, and an engine of opportunity for the family that follow in your path. With help from advisors, follow these steps to move downfield toward a future dance in the end zone:

1)   Answer the Seven Essential Questions (Chapter Two)

2)   Take prudent risk management steps (Chapter Three)

3)   Reduce your Exit Magic Number (Chapter Four)

4)   Set your game plan for addressing the issues most Passers face (this Chapter)

Key Points for Passers:

- Are you ready to bet your retirement on your child?

- Separate control of your business from ownership of your business to assist in the orderly transfer of both.

- The more you expect your business to grow in the future, the sooner you must get started. A growing business owned by you increases potential taxes.

- When meeting the needs heirs not active in the business, remember fair is not equal and equal is not fair.

- Insure your estate has liquidity for taxes, debt or other needs.

Proceed to the last two chapters (starting on page 174) to address life after exit and finish your game plan for dancing in the end zone.

6

The Outie's Game Plan

Selling your business to a third party for top dollar is a dream achievement for Outies. Sale to a third party provides more than a potential path to financial freedom. Sale to a third party is personally rewarding— somebody else believes your business is worth as much as you do. Selling may fulfill a business legacy if customers, employees and perhaps even the company name continue forward because of your efforts and accomplishment.

Most owners know that they cannot simply *assume* somebody will buy the business when they want for as much as they want. Have you ever considered what makes a business more sellable and what might make it less so? In my experience, nearly all intermediaries (professionals who sell businesses for a living) will acknowledge two things about selling businesses. First, they try to select businesses they believe are most likely to sell because their compensation is predominantly tied to the business sale (a "success" fee). Second, the best intermediaries typically sell only one-half to two-thirds of the businesses they represent. How come expert intermediaries, choosing the most sellable businesses from among dozens or hundreds and financially motivated to make the sale, only sell about one in two or three businesses? What makes one business more desirable to a buyer than another?

This is a critical question for Outies, and the answer is often not what you might expect. Many owners fall into the trap of thinking their business's attractiveness is based solely on the business's financials—a sort of "If you build it profitably, they will come" way of thinking. Profits and other financial results are important to an outside buyer, but by no means represent the whole story. Outies who want to sell their business for the maximum value, at a time of their choosing and for the greatest after-tax results, have to carefully consider more than the business's bottom line.

This chapter focuses on what Outies must do to get those results. The first four chapters provided an exit planning foundation for all business owners. From here, we focus on the Outie's game plan. Most Outies need to address the following issues:

1) Building Transferable Value

2) Anticipating Your Buyer's Wants

3) Favorably Aligning the Three Ts: Timing, Terms and Taxes

Issue One: Building Transferable Value

Many Outies dream one day someone will walk in, drop a large check on the desk and tell them to go hit the beach or break out the golf clubs. Unfortunately it usually does not work this way. Selling a closely-held business, even a good business, is a challenge. Too many owners reach their ideal exit age only to realize they have made a massive mistake—they allowed their business to become more valuable to them than to anybody else. In other words, the business's value is not easily or fully *transferable* to another party. If a potential buyer perceives that your business's value cannot be safely and cost-effectively transferred, then that party is not likely to write a significant check.

Let's consider some examples. If you are the business's most key employee, transferrable value is undermined. If your business's highly efficient operations are not documented, it will be difficult for a buyer to cost-effectively leverage those operations. If your long term customers have always done business on just a handshake without formal contracts or agreements, it's harder for a buyer to transfer these relationships. If your strong financial results are not reflected in financial statements that a buyer can readily understand, we've undermined transferrable value. Building transferable value may require growing your business in a different manner because it's not just about what has worked up to this point for you.

There are certain conditions that enhance a business's transferable value. We call these Enhancers. Most Enhancers do not immediately increase revenues or profits, although over time they often will. Enhancers increase transferable value by reducing potential risk for the buyer. Buyers want to know not only what your business has accomplished, but also *how* the business accomplished those results. The more confidence a potential buyer has in how your business works, the less the buyer will fear the business falters after your exit. For example:

- If your business is more profitable than industry averages, how did it get that way?

- If your operations are exceedingly efficient, how do they work?

- If revenues are up double digit percentages every year, how did you achieve this?

What your business has done up to this point is history. Buyers only use history as a guide; they will not pay for it. Buyers open up the checkbook for expected future results. How much risk buyers perceive surrounding those future results depends on how well they can leverage the way your business works. If you grow your business paying attention only to results and not how you got them, you likely create a business that is worth more to you than to anybody else, a business that lacks transferable value. The following plays for your Playbook are designed to help enhance the business's transferable value:

Playbook: Business Growth Plan

Why would a book on exit planning suggest implementing a business growth plan? Isn't this a book about how to get out? Well, for an Outie to get out somebody else must want to get in—and be willing to write a check in the process. If you don't have a viable plan for growing the business, then one of two things likely happens, both of which are bad. One, a potential buyer also will not know how to grow the business, and will walk away. Two, the buyer will see a way to grow your business that you did not, and will likely buy the business for less than what you could have received because they saw something you missed.

Don't leave it up to others to figure out how your business grows after your exit. Mapping out your business's growth plan enhances transferable value. A growth plan also helps prevent against the natural tendency to become stagnant as you get closer to exit. Consider including in your growth plan:

- Three to five ideas that could accelerate your business's growth, and a plan of action to implement those ideas.

- A summary of your business's competitive advantages and how they may be sustained and leveraged going forward.

- A five year pro forma financial model that gives buyers confidence in the results.

Paint a credible picture of a bright future so your buyer will pay you a premium for those future results.

Playbook: Readable and Reliable Financial Statements

Transferable value can be weakened if outside parties cannot read your business's financial statements or do not trust their accuracy. We see this occur in a couple situations. One, you ignore your financial statements because you run your business by experience and intuition. The statements suffer from neglect and bear little relevance to business reality and decisions. In another situation, financial statements are closely maintained and constantly referenced, but are so tailored to your business's specifics that they are undecipherable by an outside party. Owners will say "My business is different from most others so our financials have to…" This is dangerous ground. Your financial statements may become so unconventional that a potential buyer may become confused, or may be unwilling to learn your homemade language.

Many advisors suggest "cleaning up" financial statements shortly before you exit. I disagree. Keep accurate and conventional statements from now forward. As we have discussed, prepare for a buyer to come along at any time. Even if that does not happen, accurate statements should help make sound decisions and build transferable value. Review with your exit planning team the following questions:

- How would a likely buyer react to your current financial statements?

- Are special points and issues accurately reflected in the footnotes?

- Do your statements accurately convey the business's financial strengths? If not, why not?

- What are your weakest financial areas? How should you address these weaknesses?

Discuss with your advisors how your statements should be prepared prior to sale. Most potential buyers will review your financial statements with a microscope. Generally at least two years of audited statements is advisable prior to sale.*

Playbook: Document How Your Business Works

Your business has a certain way that it works. If the business has been successful up to this point, things are working well. If the way your business works—its operational processes, marketing tactics, selling techniques, planning methods, etc.—reside solely in your head or the heads of your employees, transferable value decreases because a buyer's potential risk has increased. Undocumented business processes are not easily scalable, sustainable or transferable.

Document how your business works. Walk around and look at it as an outside buyer would. Are all your important processes such as accounts receivable, sales, marketing, customer service and production written down? If not, get your team recording them in an orderly manner and stored in a convenient and accessible format. This may improve transferable value and help grow your business in an efficient and profitable manner between now and exit. Well documented operations assist in unifying your internal processes, increase consistency and facilitate training. This is another example of how a better managed business helps create a successful exit, and how exit planning helps create a better business today.

Playbook: Intellectual Property

Intellectual property such as business brand, trademarks, servicemarks and copyrights are the wildcard of transferable value—it may have little impact on transferable value or you may hit the jackpot. Intellectual property can separate your business from the rest of the crowd. Buyers may pay extra for what your business has that nobody else does. Just like the lottery, if you do not play then you have no chance of winning.

You do not need a large household name company to build intellectual property value. In specific markets, industries and geographies it's possible to create unique value. Meet with an intellectual property attorney who can advise how to create transferable value in this area. If you believe a buyer

---

* There are three levels of financial statements: *Compiled* statements are prepared by an outside accountant but solely based on numbers provided by you. The accountant provides no assurance of accuracy or conformity with appropriate accounting rules and conventions. *Reviewed* statements have been spot-checked by the accountants for accuracy and conformity with necessary accounting conventions. *Audited* statements have been prepared and verified by the accountants who will issue a written opinion on the accuracy and conformity.

might want your business's identity, verify that your business name and logo does not infringe upon another's. Don't risk learning during the buyer's due diligence that your business's name is a potential liability. Develop a plan for creating and protecting intellectual property.

The EZ Solution

Mark owned a successful commercial electric supply business called EZ Supply with a strong reputation in his local markets. He anticipated that a buyer would likely want to leverage his business's strong local reputation. He met with an intellectual property attorney to discuss federally registering his business name in anticipation of selling his business in the future. The attorney's research revealed four other businesses in his industry from around the country had been using a similar or the same name as EZ Supply, giving them protected status.

The attorney and Mark devised a solution. They developed a strategy to build value around a custom electrical product that Mark's business manufactured. Their efforts created regional and later national recognition for the product, diminishing the importance of Mark's business's name.

While there is no guarantee an intellectual property strategy will succeed, it only takes one buyer to covet your protected brand, patent, trademark or copyright for you to potentially receive a high price at sale.

Playbook: Desirable Contracts

Most businesses have contracts with a variety of parties: customers, suppliers, vendors, landlords and employees. Review your contracts from the perspective of a likely buyer. Are the current contracts desirable from a buyer's standpoint, or could a buyer view any of the contracts as a liability? For example, if contracts with customers are not transferable and assumable, then your potential buyer may need to approach customers and rewrite those contracts. This increases the buyer's risk of losing customers in the transition, and decreases your transferable value. Organize and review the business's current contracts and anticipate a potential buyer's needs. Evaluate future contracts based on what is best for your business's growth needs and what builds transferable value.

Playbook: Diversified Customer Base

Many closely-held businesses receive a large portion of revenue from a small percentage of customers or sources. It's an easy business decision to take on the huge new account, but it is not necessarily a helpful exit decision. Customer overconcentration presents risk to buyers—if those few customers scale back or leave, the business may be in trouble. Overconcentration is a serious value reducer; potential buyers may shy away or your business may suffer a reduced multiple at sale.

Ideally no single customer should exceed 10% of the top or bottom line. If your business struggles with this, develop a concentrated sales and marketing plan to diversify customers. Revenue increases from new or existing smaller customers may raise your sale price more than revenue increases from your largest customers.

Playbook: Upside Down Organizational Chart

To get paid the maximum value and achieve legacy goals, your business must be able to function without you. It has to be able to grow, perform and overcome challenges independent of your leadership and involvement. Otherwise, a buyer will see a business that cannot grow and may wither after your exit. Put simply, *nobody will buy your job.*

There are two parts to this tactic. First, make sure you have an accurate and sensible organizational chart. It's difficult to convey to a buyer your management team's structure and value without an accurate organizational chart. Second, place your name at the bottom—turn it upside down relative to today. Can your business perform without you at the top?

Identify your roles and responsibilities and write a plan to shift them to others in an orderly manner. This is hard for many successful owners. If left to their own devices, many owners keep doing those things they are good at and enjoy. You genuinely may be the best person for a particular job in the business because of your talent and experience. The longer you remain the best person for that job, it becomes a weakness not a strength. Even if your organization runs profitably and smoothly on a day-to-day basis without you, carefully consider how well the team would function if you were permanently gone.

The Glue That Holds It Together

When we first met James he owned a highly profitable niche manufacturing business. Gross profits were high and he had low overhead. His business had few competitors. James's top four employees ran the business with little input. James frequently traveled for a month, came back for a week and then left again for another month. Business was good, and increasingly he was interested in selling.

We discussed his business and its many attractive attributes. But when we came to his key people, James said, "Well, that may be a problem." I was surprised. Clearly his employees were running his business without James.

"They do run the business," he confirmed. "But without me they might kill each other. They don't get along. When I get back from trips I spend the first few days doing nothing but resolve conflicts. If I were totally gone several of them might quit. It's not that I am greatest guy in the world, but I'm the glue that holds them together."

Reducing your contribution as an employee not only builds transferable value, it helps build a better business. A business that grows without its owner probably has a strong management team, a clear mission and effective operations. The sooner you turn upside your organizational chart the quicker you create this result.

Playbook: Normalized Earnings

Most owners do not like paying income taxes each year. To lessen the tax bite, owners often reduce business taxable profits by maximizing personal compensation and employment-related perks. To avoid understating your profits at time of sale, standard practice is to "normalize" financial statements and add back in those expenses that a buyer probably would discontinue. "Add-backs" may include:

- Above market owner compensation

- Profit sharing and other retirement plan contributions

- Compensation paid to working family members

- Top rate rent paid for assets you own outside the business and lease back such as the commercial office building

- Club memberships

- Business travel in generous accommodations

- Expensive automotive leases

Consider going through the exercise of recasting your financials now, regardless how far away your target exit age. Minimizing profits for tax planning year after year eventually clouds the true picture of your business's full financial capacity. It's not unusual that add-backs increase disclosed profits by 50% to 100%. Growing your business without periodically measuring its full profit potential is a like balancing a checkbook only looking at half the deposits. Furthermore, you are not in complete control of when you will exit. Waiting to normalize your earnings until you are "ready" falls under the Fallacy of Five Years. If an opportunity to sell comes along sooner than expected, you will have to scramble. Normalizing close to the time of sale may confuse a buyer as to the full historical profits of the business. Without adequate records, it will be difficult to clearly answer which expenses were "extra" and which were not four or five years earlier. If a surprise buyer does not come along, maximize the reported profits on your business income tax returns during your last few years until your target exit age. You will pay more taxes during those final years, but you may get those dollars back in the form of a higher sale price.

Issue Two: Anticipating Your Buyer's Wants

Passers and Innies often know exactly who their successor will be—the person or group of people that already works for them. Squeezers do not need a buyer. Only Outies usually have no idea who will purchase their business until the end. While your buyer's name may not be known at this time, a profile of likely buyers often can be formulated. Anticipating your possible buyer and its wants opens the door to maximizing your business's sale price.* For example, if a buyer craves your business's location, focus on dominating local markets. If you anticipate a buyer will want your management team, hire a crack team that is young enough to keep working

---

* For simplicity, we will assume your buyer is an organization such as another business or investment group and use the pronoun "it". Of course a buyer could be a group of people or single individual.

past your exit date. If a buyer will want your proprietary products, maximize brand value.

Your exit planning team, and specifically an "intermediary", can help. The term intermediary includes a broad spectrum of professionals who help buy and sell closely-held businesses. Generally speaking, "business brokers" take a listing-based approach (much like a real estate agent) and work with businesses up to a few million dollars in value. For larger businesses the titles change to "investment banker" or "mergers and acquisitions" specialist. These professionals create a controlled-auction in the hope that multiple buyers compete to write you a check. An experienced intermediary often can isolate the profile of a likely buyer.

Different types of buyers want different things. Smaller closely-held businesses (generally up to a few million dollars) are usually purchased by individuals who want a business they can personally lead. The more comfortable they are running this business on their own, the more attractive it may be.

With larger businesses, it becomes more likely your buyer is another organization rather than an individual. Expect this organization to be a sophisticated, experienced shopper that knows exactly what it wants, or has hired sophisticated, experienced advisors to guide it. The buyer may look at dozens of businesses before settling on its next target. Buyers of medium to large businesses fall into two main types:

Financial Buyers

Financial buyers focus on the rate of return your business offers as an investment opportunity. Private equity groups, or PEGs, are a common financial buyer. PEGs purchase businesses using a combination of debt and their own cash. Financial buyers want businesses with competent management and potential for exponential growth. These buyers may purchase all of the business or just a portion. If it's a partial transaction, they will expect the management team—usually including you—to stay and grow the business for three to five years, after which time the rest of the business will be sold. This two-part transaction is commonly called a "private recapitalization". Private recapitalizations can achieve a bigger financial win for you if the business grows significantly between the first and second sale.

A financial buyer may be willing to do the deal without you if the remaining management team can grow the business. This is commonly called a management buy-out (MBO). The more capable your management team, the more this may be an option. Otherwise, prepare to commit to a three to five year sprint to grow the business. Depending on how much of the business you sell upfront, you may lose control and many of the personal freedoms you enjoyed when you did not have a boss.

Strategic Buyers

Financial buyers look for the best rate of return. Strategic buyers look for *synergy*. They believe that parts or all of your business added onto their business creates dramatically better results. In short, your one plus their four will equal seven. The greater the synergy your buyer perceives, the higher the possible price. Strategic buyers may want the product or service line, technology, customer list, geographic markets or other pieces of your business.

Strategic buyers usually are another business already in your industry or one that wishes to expand into your industry. To anticipate their wants, consider your industry trends and compare your business's strengths. Evaluate the greatest synergistic opportunities your business offers a strategic buyer. Often it's possible to narrow the scope of buyers down to a target list. For example, size is an important factor. A general rule of thumb is a prospective strategic buyer will be three to four times larger than your business. Any smaller and the buyer's business may not be able to afford the purchase. Any larger and your business becomes too small to warrant their attention.

A strategic buyer may be less concerned how long you stick around after selling than a financial buyer. One of the possible disadvantages of a strategic buyer is your business may not continue as a standalone entity after you exit depending on the buyer's intentions.

Initial Public Offerings (IPOs)

Rather than finding a single buyer, it's possible to sell to the open market in an initial public offering (IPO). "Going public" can be an exciting exit strategy for the successful owner. This option may bring instant liquidity and a premium price. Exiting via IPO is only for larger closely-held businesses: the legal, tax and other costs can approach seven figures. An IPO is not for everyone. Your business would operate under public scrutiny and be subject to a myriad of regulations and reporting requirements. (Some CEOs of publicly traded businesses admit they wish they were closely-held!) Discuss with your advisors if this option may fit your exit plans.

Issue Three: Aligning in Your Favor the Three Ts: Timing, Terms and Taxes

When the topic of selling the business comes up, many owners focus on the gross price they believe their business is worth and pay attention to little else. "My business is worth $XX million, and I won't think about selling for less," is a common sentiment. With respect to your business, two numbers are more important than the gross sale price. The first is your Exit Magic Number, because it represents how much you *need* and not how much you want in order to achieve financial freedom. The other is the net amount you receive from selling your business, not the gross. As the accountant's old saying goes: "Top line is vanity. Bottom line is sanity." (Don't forget the last part: "Cash is reality.")

Typically the biggest culprit pulling down the gross to the net will be taxes. Outies need to position the business to legally minimize tax erosion at sale. Generally, the timing (when you get paid) and the terms (how you get paid) determine the taxes (what the IRS gets paid) at sale. These are the "Three T's" of selling your business. Generally Outies desire to be taxed under long term capital gains rates because they are lower than ordinary income rates in most cases.* Before we can examine tactics that minimize taxes, we must review the fundamental issue of selling assets versus stock.

A Quick Comparison of Asset Sales and Stock Sales

If your business is a corporation†, you and the buyer will have to determine if the transaction will involve the business's stock or its assets. The difference is simple. The buyer may purchase your shares of stock directly from you, or the buyer may purchase from the business assets such as customers, accounts receivable, equipment, goodwill, etc. At first this may seem like a mere formality, but the choice has large implications not the least of which is taxes. And it may come as no surprise that you and buyer usually want the opposite outcome. Most buyers will prefer an asset sale, and most sellers will prefer a stock sale.

---

* In many cases this is the opposite of what Innies desire, which is one of the key reasons why the two exit strategies of selling to an insider or selling to an outsider are different. Unlike most Outies, Innies often have years to preplan with their employee/buyer how to structure the timing and terms in the most tax favorable manner. Therefore Innies often use a different set of plays in the Playbook.

† LLCs and partnerships cannot elect a stock sale. There is no stock.

Buyers usually prefer an asset sale to reduce legal risk. Purchasing your stock may bring liabilities, known or unknown such as product warranties, employment disputes and environmental issues. Buyers also prefer asset sales because it lowers their tax bill. An asset sale usually allows the buyer to "step up" the value of the acquired assets and achieve greater depreciation benefits under IRS guidelines. The buyer wants to pay more for assets that depreciate quickly and less for assets that depreciate slowly or not at all. For these reasons, most closely-held business sales are asset sales.

A stock sale usually is more favorable to you, particularly if the business is a regular C corporation. Assets sales with a C corporation result in double-taxation, greatly increasing the possible tax bill. How does this happen? With an asset sale the buyer pays your corporation for the assets purchased, triggering potential taxes at the corporate level. When cash proceeds are finally distributed to you, the second potential tax is triggered at the personal level.

Owners of S corporations, partnerships and most limited liability companies (LLCs) are "pass through" entities for income tax purposes, meaning all business profits or losses are passed to your income tax return. While this eliminates the risk of double-taxation, you still risk drawing the short end of the tax straw at sale. If your business is sold as an asset sale, you and the buyer must determine how to allocate the purchase price across the assets involved. For example, assume you and your buyer agreed on a $10 million purchase price asset sale. How much of the $10 million will be applied to inventory, equipment or goodwill? The allocation determines your taxes, specifically if you pay lower long term capital gains taxes or higher ordinary income taxes. (Remember, the terms help dictate the taxes.) The IRS identifies seven broad asset classes under what is called the "residual method". At sale, you and the buyer must review the classes and allocate the price. Table 6-1 lists the seven classes and indicates what you and the buyer most commonly prefer for tax purposes.

Asset sales are not always less desirable to the seller. Asset sales provide flexibility to pick and chose which assets to sell and keep. If you have any shareholder loans, they may be repaid and usually the loan principal will be tax free. The issue is complicated and requires that you work with competent advisors and formulate your plan well before exit.

Table 6-1: Residual Method Asset Classes

Asset Class	Examples	What the Buyer Usually Wants	What the Seller Usually Wants
I. Cash	Cash, checking accounts, money market accounts	No preference	No preference
II. Securities	CDs, bonds, marketable securities	No preference	No preference
III. Accounts Receivable	Current and likely collectable accounts receivable (many buyers will exclude receivables significantly past due)	No preference	No preference
IV. Inventory	Goods on hand for sale (many buyers will exclude obsolete inventory)	Prefer to allocate a higher amount	Prefer to allocate a lower amount
V. Other Tangible Property	Real estate, equipment, furnishings	With real estate prefer to allocate a lower amount; other personal property prefer to allocate a higher amount	With real estate prefer to allocate a higher amount; other personal property prefer to allocate a lower amount
VI. Intangible Property	Covenants not to compete, patents, trademarks, copyrights, licenses	Prefer to allocate a lower amounts	For covenants not to compete, prefer to allocate a higher amount if a C corp or a lower amount if another business form; for other property prefer to allocate a higher amount
VII. Goodwill & Going Concern Value	Value of the business not allocated to a prior Class	Prefer to allocate a lower amount	Prefer to allocate a higher amount

The following tactics may help you and your advisors position the business to achieve the most favorable timing, terms and taxes at sale.

Playbook: Tax Analysis and Plan

Ask your advisors to review and analyze the tax impact of your business sale now. Don't wait until you are on the verge of selling to examine and understand your tax picture. That's not much different than waiting until April 14th to discuss with your CPA what can be done about reducing income taxes. Owners must plan far ahead to consciously grow their business toward a tax-efficient exit.

This tactic is surprisingly simple and frequently unused. In research for this book, we found that less than 10% of business owners had a written analysis of their exit's tax impact.[*] Your advisors can provide reasonable scenarios and discuss the forecasted results. Assume an asset sale because that's the more common form and it's possibly a worse-case scenario for taxes. With an understanding of how taxes look today, consider strategies to build tax-efficient value going forward.

Playbook: Ideal Legal Business Entities

The type of legal entity your business uses has a large impact on the tax bill at sale. Is your business a regular C corporation, a subchapter S corporation, a partnership, an LLC or other form? Or are business operations and assets divided up into several entities of different types? When you founded your business, how the legal entity would impact taxes at sale may not have been on your mind. Even if you had taken taxes into consideration, tax laws and other factors may have changed since then and made previous assumptions obsolete. Outies must select the type(s) of legal entities that provide the most favorable tax outcome.

While it is not possible to provide a one-size-fits-all answer on which entity is best, commonly a regular C corporation is the least tax favorable form for Outies.[†] Outies with C corporations face potential double-taxation if

---

[*] 2008 White Horse Advisors Survey of Closely-Held Business Owners

[†] An important exception is if you intend to sell your business to an employee stock ownership plan (ESOP). An ESOP is a vehicle to sell the business to insider key employees, making the owner an Innie. See Chapter Seven for more on Innies and ESOPs.

an asset sale.* Even if you exit via a stock sale, your buyer may discount the price to adjust for the tax savings it forfeits under a stock sale. In the following example, assume an asset sale of a $10 million business with zero tax basis. The results are significant as shown in Table 6-2.

Table 6-2: C Corporation vs S Corporation Asset Sale

	C Corporation	S Corporation
Asset sale value	$10 million	$10 million
Corporate tax @20%	- $2.0 million	n/a
Personal tax @20%	- $1.6 million	- $2.0 million
Net to owner	$6.4 million	$8.0 million
Figures are hypothetical.		

If your business is a regular C corporation, the following plays may reduce the risk of double-taxation. If your business is not a C corporation, consider jumping ahead to the play called Charitable Remainder Trust found on page 142.

Playbook: Convert Your C Corporation to an S Corporation

Perhaps the most obvious option for C corporation owners is converting to another legal form, commonly an S corporation. Converting from C to S to minimize taxes at sale can take time. When a C is converted to an S and sold within ten years after the conversion, a special tax called a built-in gains tax may apply at the highest corporate rate. Sales ten years or more after conversion usually avoid double-taxation. In general, built-in gains tax can be minimized by having the business valued as of the date of the S conversion. Converting to an S corporation when profits are low may reduce the potential tax. The more time you have to consider this tactic then the more favorable results you may achieve.

---

* If you are not sure of the difference, a C corporation pays its own income taxes. S corporations pay no income taxes but rather pass through all income or losses to the shareholders in proportion to ownership. C corporations file an 1120 income tax return while S corporations file an 1120S. Many closely-held businesses founded in the early 1980's and earlier are still C corporations because prior to several tax law change in the mid and late 1980's S corporations were rarely used.

Playbook: Personal Goodwill

C corporation asset sales risk double taxation because the buyer purchases assets from the business, creating the first tax. (Taking the cash out of the business creates the second tax.) One technique to minimize double-taxation is to demonstrate that the asset being sold does not reside in the corporation but rather in you the business owner. Called Personal Goodwill, this tactic may benefit smaller closely-held businesses where the owner is heavily engaged in the business. If the buyer pays you for your "personal goodwill" rather than the business, then the payments are only subject to one level of taxation. A buyer usually will not care if the "goodwill" is business or personal as it's treated for tax purposes.[*]

Personal goodwill requires that your talents, relationships and skills are the real source of value and not the business itself. (This is the opposite of turning your organizational chart upside down as discussed earlier in this chapter.) The more your business depends on you then the greater the potential personal goodwill. Table 6-3 shows some of the considerations behind asserting personal goodwill:

Table 6-3: Business Goodwill vs. Personal Goodwill

It may be business goodwill if...	It may be personal goodwill if....
The business operates effectively beyond the owner's skills and relationships.	The business is highly dependent on owner's skills and relationships.
Before the sale, a covenant not to compete or similar restrictions are in place between the business and the owner.	Before the sale, the owner does not have a covenant not to compete or similar restriction with the business.
The business has some owners not actively involved in the business.	All owners are actively involved in the business.
Customer relationships are largely independent of the owner's involvement.	Customer relationships largely tied to the owner.
Delivering the business's services and products occurs largely without the involvement of the owner.	Delivering the business's services and products is largely dependent upon the owner's involvement.

---

[*] Business goodwill or personal goodwill are both amortized over 15 years by the buyer.

Personal goodwill becomes harder to argue as the business grows larger because businesses typically become more self-sustaining with size. If you incorporate personal goodwill in the terms of sale, use separate purchase agreements for business assets and the personal goodwill. The buyer will commonly insist on an employment agreement or non-compete covenant (or similar restrictions) if personal goodwill is purchased.

In its essence, personal goodwill argues that the business is worth *less* in order to minimize taxes. It's a powerful example of why Outies should not fixate on the potential "maximum value" of the business but rather on your Exit Magic Number and the net result from the sale.

Playbook: Section 1202

Personal goodwill is a tactic based on facts and circumstances. Another tactic is based on the tax code. Under Section 1202, you may be eligible to exclude 50% the taxable gain realized when you sell the business, up to $10 million or ten times your basis in the stock, whichever amount is greater. Some of the requirements include:

- Your business must be a C corporation.

- The stock must have been issued after August 11, 1993 and you must have held it for longer than five years.

- The aggregate gross assets of the corporation must have been less than $50 million at the time of and immediately after issuing the stock.

- Your business must be involved in certain industries such as manufacturing, wholesaling and retailing. Farming and many service industries are excluded.

Unfortunately, some of benefits from Section 1202 may be eroded if you are subject to alternative minimum taxes. A careful review of your tax situation is required.

Playbook: NewCo

One additional tactic for Outies with C corporations is to shift business revenues, profits and assets to a new legal entity ("newco") created alongside the existing C corporation. The idea is to build value in the new business entity, typically an S corporation or LLC, while freezing or reducing the value tied up in the existing C corporation.

This tactic may require many years to implement. Customers, operations, employees and capital typically cannot be moved with the flip of a switch. Outside parties such as bankers, customers and suppliers may need to be consulted. Operating two businesses side-by-side for several years increases overhead costs and administrative workload. Despite this, shifting value away from the regular C corporation may outweigh the costs and burden.

The following techniques may help favorably align the Three Ts (Timing, Terms and Taxes) regardless of the type of business entity you use.

Playbook: Charitable Remainder Trust (CRT)

Charitable Remainder Trusts can create significant tax savings for Outies with any type of business entity, especially if you face a large potential tax bill at sale. With a CRT, your first step is not selling the business but giving it a charitable trust. However you keep an income stream that is paid back to you for a defined period of time such as the duration of your life. (This is your "remainder" interest.) If the income stream is fixed, this is called a Charitable Remainder Annuity Trust.* Funds to make the payments back to you come from the trust assets, either the business's earnings or proceeds from the business sale once it is sold. At the end of the specified time period, usually your death, the business or remaining assets pass to the trust beneficiary which must be a tax-exempt charitable institution. Some of the advantages CRTs offer include:

- You may create larger payments back to you than would be possible if you had sold the business on your own. If your business is worth $10 million, at sale you owe $2 million (assuming 20% long term capital gains) leaving $8 million left to invest for your income needs. If you donate the business to the CRT and it sells the business for $10 million, the capital gains tax bill is $0 because a charitable trust pays no income taxes. All $10 million may be invested to produce income for you. Assuming a 5% return on the proceeds, the annual income is

---

* A variation is a CRUT, which is a Charitable Remainder UniTrust. In a CRUT, the payments are not fixed like in a Charitable Remainder Annuity Trust but rather are a percentage of the trust's assets. This creates flexibility to change payments as the trust assets change in value over time. However, it also creates the need to appraise the business's value each year. Consult with your advisors about other variations as well.

$500,000 using the CRT compared to $400,000 selling the business on your own.

- Often most of the distributions from the trust back to you will be taxed at favorable capital gains rates.

- The entire value of the business is removed from your taxable estate, reducing potential estate taxes.

- Your charitable gift usually creates an income tax deduction. However, the deduction is not the full value of your business but is reduced by the value of the remainder interest (basically the business value minus the payments back to you) based on IRS tables. Also you may not be able to use all of the charitable deductions; there are annual limitations and unused deductions may be carried forward only five years.

CRTs are complex and require detailed preparations, not least of which is finding a charity that will partner with you. Generally once you donate the business to the CRT you may no longer work in the business, although it is possible you could serve as consultant. Some owners hesitate to consider CRTs because they do not want to give away their largest asset and leave little for their heirs. One solution is to use some of the payments from the charitable trust to purchase life insurance owned in an irrevocable "Wealth Replacement Trust" to replace a portion of the business's value. If properly structured this trust may provide heirs with income tax and estate tax free proceeds.

Playbook: Stock Swap

The buyer of your business may be another business, and it may offer you its stock at sale in lieu of cash. If this transaction meets the definition of a "swap" under the law rather than a sale, then taxes are not triggered because you merely exchanged your asset for another of presumably equal value. Your taxes are deferred until you eventually sell that stock. Deferring a tax bill is nearly always advantageous—in essence you enjoy an interest-free loan from the IRS until the taxes are due. Two of the essential requirements to qualify for a stock swap include:

- You must receive voting stock in the buyer's business.

- The buyer must purchase at least 80% of each and every class of stock in your business.

While tax attractive, the tactic can be risky from an investment standpoint. You are exchanging your business for a portion of the buyer's business. There are tactics to reduce the investment risk if your buyer is a publicly traded stock. Also verify if you are receiving restricted or unrestricted stock. Restricted stock is generally not permitted to be sold after the swap for a period of time such as two or three years.

Playbook: Royalties and Earnouts

Royalties and earnouts are sale terms other than cash that may be part of your transaction. A royalty agreement pays additional dollars if sales or profits from a specific product or service exceed certain benchmarks. Earnouts usually are tied to overall business performance. After the sale, if the business's results are better than agreed benchmarks you receive additional payments Royalties and earnouts are commonly used if you and the buyer have a different view of the future. For example, you may believe the business's growth and performance will accelerate in the near future, faster than recent history suggests. Perhaps you recently implemented new technology or expanded a product line. The buyer may be less convinced, or at least unwilling to pay for unproven results. In this situation, consider owning that product or service separately from the business. If the product or service has that much untapped potential but the buyer has doubts, keep it and determine a separate exit strategy for that asset.

Unfortunately, royalties and earnouts too often are used because the buyer recognizes a weakness in the business. The buyer is unwilling to pay without contingencies for fear the business may decline after you sell. If contingent payments are included in the sale terms, the outgoing owner may resent the performance requirements or be unwilling to play the role of a dutiful employee. The earnout or royalty may be doomed from the start should any of this occur.

Carefully and clearly determine the earnout or royalty schedule, benchmarks and other parameters. If after selling the business you no longer have control, consider tying earnouts to gross revenues rather than bottom line profits. Consider including royalties or earnouts in your sale terms only if they meet your needs.

Playbook: Employment Contracts

Employment contracts are another potential technique to align the terms of the sale in your favor. Many buyers want a post-sale employment period to reduce risks of a rough transition or a business that declines without you.

(The less valuable of an employee you are to the business, the less risk your buyer will perceive.) While it's better to have a business than runs without you, an employment contract can benefit you. Under the contract the business can provide reasonable perks and benefits that otherwise you must purchase using after-tax dollars. You also might enjoy your roles and responsibilities under the agreement, assuming you are comfortable working for the new owner.

The employment agreement should not be part of the sale agreement. If the employment agreement is bundled in with the sale agreement, should you quit employment the whole transaction could be attacked by the buyer for non-performance. It is important to remember that income received under an employment contract is taxed under ordinary tax rates.

Playbook: Consulting Company

A buyer may want you to remain engaged with the business for a period of time as a consultant rather than employee. You may enjoy the role and flexibility afforded a consult. A downside to an employment contract is the income you receive will be taxed under ordinary income tax rates.

Set up a consulting company to contract for and deliver the services rather than personally delivering the services. There are several advantages:

- If you do not immediately need or want the income earned, evaluate a tax deductible retirement plan inside the consulting company to shelter earnings from income taxes.

- Consider setting up your consulting business as a C corporation to provide you with employee benefits such as medical insurance or private long term care insurance in a tax favorable manner.

- Establishing a consulting company allows you to hire out to another party the work of delivering those services.

- If your health deteriorated or if you die prematurely, any unfulfilled services could be delivered by another party hired out by the consulting business. Otherwise unearned revenues could be forfeited.

Conclusion

Successfully exiting from your business via a third party sale can be your crowning achievement as a business owner. If financial freedom is secured, and if you have peace of mind about family, employees and customers, your exit probably will be a success. With help from advisors, follow these steps to move downfield toward a future dance in the end zone:

1) Answer the Seven Essential Question (Chapter Two)

2) Take prudent risk management steps (Chapter Three)

3) Reduce your Exit Magic Number (Chapter Four)

4) Set your game plan for meeting the issues most Outies face (this Chapter)

Key Points for Outies:

- Just because your business makes money does not mean it will sell for maximum value.

- Owners get trapped when their business is worth more to them than to any other party. To sell your business you must grow <u>transferable</u> value.

- Enhance transferable value by carefully considering how your business works so that a buyer will perceive less risk of diminished results after you exit.

- Anticipate your likely buyers' profile and grow the transferable value the buyer may want.

- Align the Three T's of selling your business: Timing, Terms and Taxes in your favor to reduce tax erosion at sale.

Proceed to the last two chapters (starting on page 174) to address life after exit and finish your game plan for dancing in the end zone.

7

The Innie's Game Plan

Selling your business to one or more top employees may be deeply rewarding. Long term, valued employees become like extended family. To see the business continue forward under leadership you selected and groomed acknowledges all your efforts and extends the business legacy. Rewards can include the financial realm—top employees may be the best, and in some cases the only, potential buyer. They know the business and would rather own it after you exit than go to work for somebody else. Top employees usually possess strong emotional ties to the business and are enthusiastic about the future. Their first hand experience with operations, customers, suppliers and employees helps achieve orderly transitions.

There are practical advantages to selling to your top employees. (For simplicity we will assume from this point forward you are selling to a small group of senior employees unless otherwise noted.) You probably know their strengths and weaknesses, whereas outside buyers are likely to be strangers. Also, Innies and their top employees may pursue a careful and gradual transition of ownership and control, helping reassure customers, lenders and other employees. Many outside buyers would not agree to such a protracted changing of the guard. Last, selling to insiders solves one of the biggest problems Outies face—finding a buyer. Your buyers already work for you.

Despite these advantages, successfully selling to top employees can be difficult. Perhaps the biggest reason is cash; top employees usually do not have any. If your key employees had any money they would not be your key employees. Worse, they usually lack collateral to raise capital on their own. Outside buyers can bring their own cash to the closing table. The only source of cash available to top employees is the very business you are selling to them. Innies need to figure out how to sell to employees who have no cash in a tax efficient and low risk manner.*

Another challenge for Innies is holding onto top employees until you are ready to sell. A talented, top-performing employee who aspires to be a business owner may not wait five, ten or twenty years until you are ready to exit. Competitors may lure them away. An employee could become disabled or die prematurely. (In most situations, an employee's retirement should not be a threat. The employees you have in mind to buy your business typically are younger than you and unlikely to retire before your exit.) Losing a top employee for any reason creates a double negative for Innies—you lose that employee's current efforts and a future buyer. Exiting via sale to employees has a unique set of advantages and disadvantages:

Table 7-1: Selling to Your Employee(s)

Potential Advantages	Potential Disadvantages
The buyers are identified.	Employees typically have no cash.
Employees have experience and familiarity with the businesses.	Loss of top employees before the transition.
Current owners have direct experience with their top employees' talents and abilities.	Potential awkwardness of excluding some members of the team from the transaction.
The opportunity to plan for transition over an extended time.	

* In some cases, usually with medium to larger closely-held businesses, top employees may be able to bring cash to the closing table through the backing of an outside financier such as a private equity group (PEG). Commonly called a management buy-out (MBO), these transactions share many of the characteristics of selling to an outside third party. If this may be an option for your business, consider also reading Chapter Six: The Outie's Game Plan. You and your advisors can determine which tactics from the Playbook best fit your situation.

The first four chapters provided an exit planning foundation for all business owners. From here, we focus on the Innie's game plan. Most Innies need to address the following issues in order to dance in the end zone:

1) Transferring Control in an Orderly Manner

2) Favorably Aligning the Three Ts: Timing, Terms and Taxes

3) Reducing Default Risk

Issue One: Transferring Control in an Orderly Manner

Among the issues Innies must consider, transferring control probably needs addressed first. Many experts, books and workshops on selling to your employees jump immediately into structuring the transaction and reducing taxes. But if you have little confidence in your employees' ability to lead the business then everything else becomes moot. Your employees may have a proven track record as your management team, but putting your business and financial freedom in their hands pushes beyond confidence and into the realm of faith.

If your employees have been running the business without you for at least several years, you may be steps ahead. Few owners are that removed. Typically you play a valuable role in the business, at least on strategic matters but perhaps also on the tactical level: sales, operations, finance, etc. Unless you successfully transfer control, the end zone dance will be short or never happen. The following tactics in your Playbook can help make this happen:

Playbook: Sale to Employee(s) Feasibility Study

Engineers, architects and contractors do not erect a building without a site plan that carefully examines the land. Surgeons do not cut into a patient until exhausting every relevant medical test and scan to understand what they face. Transferring your business to top employees is arguably no less important or complex. Start with a formal assessment, commonly called a feasibility study.

A study should review the current situation and assess what it will take to transition your roles and responsibilities without adversely impacting the business or you. Some questions a study should answer include:

- What are your roles and responsibilities today? Which ones do you like and not like? (Most owners hold onto responsibilities they like.)

- What are each of the top employee's strengths and weaknesses?

- Within your top employees, who aspires to be the next CEO?

- Are there any holes or weaknesses in your management team today? If yes, how will the holes be filled?

- How will groups such as other employees, customers, suppliers and lenders react to a transition? If you anticipate concerns, what needs to be done to assure a smooth transition?

- Under what circumstances will you comfortably transfer strategic control of the business?

Innies must start now addressing this issue. Your team may not be ready, willing and able to buy your business today. One or more major obstacles usually surface. Perhaps one or two key positions need filled, or you don't have a successor CEO within the group. Three to five years, the conventional wisdom's suggested time to prepare for exit, is an incredibly short period of time to make management team changes. You have to identify, recruit, hire, acclimate and come to trust that person or group with your business and your financial freedom. And that assumes you hire or promote the correct people on the first try. If your new hires or promotions don't work out, then you must start all over again. You cannot afford par performers or unfilled positions. Starting now reduces risks and discomfort down the road:

I Haven't Slept a Wink

Judy owned a large automotive towing service chain. For years she had worked five and six days a week. When we first met Judy, she had grown tired of the effort and was determined to turn over the business to her two top employees as soon as possible. She admitted that they were not as ready as they should be, but Judy was burned out and saw that she wasn't giving the business the time and commitment it needed. Less than a year later she turned over all daily operations to these key employees.

I saw her a few weeks after making this change, and asked how she was doing. "Well," she replied with a smile, "you'd be

> so proud of me. I took a vacation with my family. I do not go to the office every day. As a matter of fact, I have not been to the office for three straight days."
>
> "That's great," I said genuinely happy for her.
>
> "No," she said, "it's not. I haven't slept a wink since."

If you have people on the team who are not ready, you must get them ready. It will not happen without your leadership and involvement. If you have people on the team who are not capable of helping you and your business reach the end zone, why wait to start making the changes that need to be made? Preparing a team that can run your business takes time, and there is no guarantee how much time you have. The longer you wait, the more difficult this may be for you, the business and them.

Playbook: Control Checkpoints

This tactic is borrowed from the Passer's Playbook. Passers (owners who want to pass the business to family) and Innies both need to pay careful attention to the orderly transfer of business control. Many Innies initially believe they have to give up control on everything all at once. That is not the case. You and your employees benefit from a carefully charted approach where control is gradually and appropriately transferred. Devise a series of Control Checkpoints that plot the path. Assign one set of responsibilities to your employees, evaluate their progress and turn over additional responsibilities only when the Checkpoints are fully met. To get started, consider the following:

- Diagram with your employees the business's organizational chart as it exists today and as it should exist going forward. Discuss your roles today and in the future.

- Together with your employees, write job descriptions and performance expectations. Identify responsibilities that you have today and prioritize which you intend to delegate and under what circumstances. Define how transfer of control is affected if one or more employees fall short of those performance expectations.

- Discuss with each employee his strengths and weaknesses. Identify a development plan for building on strengths and improving weaknesses.

- Write down the Control Checkpoints and meet monthly to measure progress and address areas that need further attention.

Playbook: One-Way Buy-Sell Plan

Before transferring control or actual ownership to employees, transfer some of the risks and responsibilities of ownership. Employees who have never been closely-held business owners may see nothing but the rewards of ownership. They probably were not in the room when you personally guaranteed the business's debt, skipped a paycheck because of tight cash or agonized over a no-win decision. They probably have not lived through the struggles and sacrifices of ownership. An excellent way to introduce some of the responsibilities of ownership is a One-Way Buy-Sell Plan. As a consultant I once heard say, business owners should "share the insomnia" with their people.

In this arrangement, enter into a buy-sell agreement with your top employees to purchase the business should you die or become disabled.[*] (The agreement is one-way because nothing happens if an employee dies or becomes disabled.) Everybody potentially benefits from this tactic. If you are disabled or die, you or your family will receive full payment for the business and employees receive the business. The agreement introduces to employees a serious and legally binding commitment—owning a business demands plenty of serious and legally binding commitments. Require the employees to pay for some to all of the insurance coverage that accompanies the legal agreement. This puts the employees' skin in the game—owning a business requires plenty of skin in the game. Two Real World Stories reveal the potential benefits of this tactic:

It's Not All Fun in the Sun

Wilson was the sole owner of a highly profitable service business. He was concerned that should he die, the business, which his family depended upon, would likely fold. Wilson had a trusted general manager named Russ. Russ was only forty years old at the time. If something happened to Wilson and the business folded, Russ would have to find a new job.

A one-way buy-sell agreement between Wilson and Russ was established. If Wilson prematurely dies or becomes disabled, Russ would use insurance to purchase the company. To share the cost of the insurance policies, Wilson paid Russ a

[*] Review Chapter Three for more on buy-sell plans.

> bonus equal to the premiums and Russ agreed to pay the income taxes on the bonus. Russ's out of pocket cost was only about $2,500 per year, but his response was, "This costs $2,500 bucks? Wow. And I thought owning a business was all fun in the sun."

If one or more of your key employees will not share in this cost, how comfortable are you that they will be willing and able to purchase the business and make prudent financial decisions once they own it? Some employees say they want ownership but may not be willing to bear the costs and risks that come with the responsibility.

Not Everybody Wants to Be an Owner

Glenn founded his technology consulting firm nearly twenty years earlier and grew it to several hundred employees. Glenn's right hand in the firm was Jack. Because Jack was nearly fifteen years younger, Glenn always believed Jack would buy him out when Glenn wanted to exit.

Glenn approached Jack about entering into a one-way buy-sell agreement to address the risk of Glenn's disability or death. Jack declined. Glenn was surprised and even hurt. Jack explained that he enjoyed everything about the firm and his relationship with Glenn, but had no aspirations to be an owner without Jack. If something was to happen to Glenn, Jack said he would help the firm and Glenn's family in any way possible but not as the new owner.

Glenn's disappointment quickly changed into relief. He had been assuming for years that Jack was part of his exit plan. Thankfully he found out early enough to find a new buyer.

Another benefit of one-way buy-sell agreements is they create an early opportunity to introduce your desire to exit via internal sale without tipping your hand on specific details such as timing. Confidentiality is important, but if you want to sell to these employees then as soon as possible it's necessary to know if they want to buy. A one-way buy-sell emphasizes that you intend to stick around for some time, otherwise why bother with the agreement? Approaching them with the agreement as a risk management tool for today opens the door to a conversation about you future exit plans.

Issue Two: Aligning in Your Favor the Three T's: Timing, Terms and Taxes

As progress in the orderly transfer of control, the challenge shifts to addressing the timing (when you get paid), terms (how you get paid) and taxes (what the IRS gets paid) of your sale. You and your employees have the opportunity to cooperate on this issue. At some point you and the employees must set a price, and of course you will want it high and they will prefer low. While two sides have different agendas on price, there is only one business. The one business will cash flow your buyout, either through payments to you or payments to a lender or an equity partner that provided the cash. You and your employees are in this together; both depend on the business to achieve their goals. And every time a business is sold a third player comes into the room—the IRS. Without advance planning, the two sides risk the IRS collecting a large tax bill relative to the business sale price.

A Quick Introduction to Taxes

A complete discussion on how taxes work when a business is bought and sold could fill another book, but a basic understanding is needed. Innies cannot afford to ignore taxes when selling to employees. The combined tax bill between you and the employees who purchase the business can easily reach 69% of the business's price. Table 6-2 illustrates how:

Table 6-2: Overview of Taxes Upon Sale of a Business

Business's gross sale price	$10.0 million
Amount the buyer needs to earn to net $10 million @ 35% assumed federal tax rate	$15.4 million
Buyer's taxes	$5.4 million
Amount seller receives	$10.0 million
Seller's long term capital gains taxes @ 15% federal rate (assuming zero cost basis)	$1.5 million
Total combined taxes	$6.9 million
Total combined taxes as a percent of the purchase price	69%

Figures are hypothetical.

This example oversimplifies matters. The taxes may be lower but they can get worse too. State income taxes and sales taxes may apply on top of the federal taxes shown here. The example assumes the seller is taxed entirely under long term capital gains treatment; ordinary income taxes may apply on a portion of the sale proceeds resulting in an even higher tax burden.

Purchasing a business is not income tax deductible. Unlike business expenses you're accustomed to deducting, purchasing a business (or its assets) is generally not a current expense but rather a capital (or "capitalized") expenditure.* The buyer can recover some taxes through depreciation and amortization expenses, but this can take a long time — fifteen years in the case of goodwill. The lost time value of money dilutes much of the impact from tax recovery through depreciation and amortization. As a consequence the business must generate up front after tax dollars to buy your interest (or pay the bank for money borrowed to buy your interest). This can be especially burdensome during the transition years immediately after your exit.

The tax impact surprises many owners, partially because not all of the taxes occur at once in most cases. In the example provided, no single year's tax return will show $5.4 million taxes paid. Taxes usually are spread out over a number of years, masking their impact. Yet if your employees purchase the business for $10 million, they need to earn about $15.4 million to net the $10 million whether they pay you directly or repay debt incurred to buy you out.

After seeing how the taxes work, some Innies conclude it's not their problem. In this example the buyer pays nearly 80% of the taxes. The combined tax bill affects you because the business's cash flow is the engine that drives the purchase — employees have no money of their own. You and your employees are in this boat together.

It's important to remember that lowering your Exit Magic Number creates flexibility to favorably align the timing, terms and taxes. Building assets and income sources outside the business prior to sale lessens financial dependency on the business. All owners have two ways to convert their business ownership into personal financial freedom: current cash and future equity. Innies must balance the two methods. Relying solely on future equity — waiting until sale to convert any significant portion of the value locked in your business — often sacrifices opportunities to reduce taxes.

---

* If you are selling a corporation, the buyers may purchase either your stock or the business's assets. There are important tax and legal differences. See Chapter Six for more on this topic.

Playbook: Sell the Business for Minimum Reasonable Value

This book does not discuss how to value a closely-held business. Part of the reason is others have adequately covered this topic, but more importantly your business's value is not the critical number. Two other numbers are more important: first is your Exit Magic Number and second is the net amount you receive for the business. Everything above the net amount is not yours. (It mostly goes to the IRS.) Owners who focus on the business's gross value often end up paying gross amounts of taxes.

If the business's gross value of your business is not paramount, and if purchasing the business is not deductible, then consider selling the business for the minimum reasonable value. Nobody is suggesting that you part with the business for a song. There are other ways to get paid besides selling the business or its assets. Change the timing (when you get paid) and terms (how you get paid) to reduce potential taxes (how much the IRS gets paid). Supplement a lower business price with one or more compensation based programs that are deductible to the business. This may reduce the total tax bill and ease the financial strain on the business, especially in early years.

Let's do the math using simple numbers to understand the basic concept. Assume you sell the business to employees for $1,000. The employees must earn about $1,540 dollars upfront (at an assumed 35% tax rate) to pay you the $1,000. Contrast this with receiving $1,000 for consulting back to the business after your exit. You still receive a gross payment of $1,000 but the consulting payment is deductible to the business in that year. To pay the $1,000 consulting fee the employees (now the new owners) only need $1,000 of cash not $1,540. It's in your best interest to get as much as you can for the business, but the business must be able to cash flow the payments (to you or to a bank).

As with any complex matter, there are disadvantages. Some important items to review with your advisors include:

- Dollars paid to you as compensation usually create ordinary income taxes and payroll taxes, which in tandem probably result in a higher total tax bill for you than long term capital gains. In many cases negotiating reasonably higher compensation offsets your higher tax burden.

- To establish a minimum justifiable minimum value for the business, consider an appraisal by a valuation expert before the sale.

- Compensation paid must be reasonable relative to the facts and circumstances.

- Your tactics must serve a bona fide business purpose. Planning well in advance helps demonstrate valid business purposes.

Consider the following compensation vehicles to supplement the sale of the business.[*]

Playbook: Employment Contract

It may be odd to think this way, but you can work at your business even after selling it. The business may pay you a reasonable amount for your role and responsibilities. The advantages of this tactic are its simplicity, the business may deduct reasonable compensation and you may keep benefits such as medical insurance, company car, etc. Earnings are subject to ordinary income taxes and payroll taxes, and you have to do real work for the compensation paid.

Establish a written employment contract that defines terms such as the compensation, employment duration and benefits to manage everybody's expectations. Also define roles and responsibilities between you and your successors to minimize misunderstanding or friction.

Playbook: Consulting Company

Instead of working as an employee, work as a consultant. The business may pay a reasonable amount for your services, often higher than what might be reasonable as an employee. The advantages include simplicity and more flexibility for you as a contractor than is often possible as an employee. You cannot access company benefits and earnings would be subject to ordinary income taxes and self-employment payroll taxes. Establish a written consulting contract and define the scope of your services so everybody has clear expectations.

Consider setting up a consulting company to contract for and deliver the services rather than you personally. There are several advantages:

- If you do not immediately need or want the income earned, evaluate a tax deductible retirement plan inside the consulting company to shelter earnings from income taxes.

- Consider setting up your consulting business as a C corporation to provide you with employee benefits such as medical insurance or private long term care insurance in a tax favorable manner.

---

[*] If you read Chapter Five: The Passer's Game Plan notice many of the plays for the Playbook are the same. Innies have much in common with Passers and share some issues and tactics.

- Establishing a consulting company allows you to hire out to another party the work of delivering those services.

- If your health deteriorated or if you die prematurely, any unfulfilled services could be delivered by another party hired out by the consulting business. Otherwise unearned revenues could be forfeited.

Playbook: Salary Continuation Plan

A salary continuation plan is a formal compensation agreement created by the business to continue an employee's salary after termination of service. Salary continuation plans are often used to honor exemplary service and motivate top employees to stay until normal retirement age. Your business may adopt a salary continuation plan that pays at your exit age. Reasonable payments usually are income tax deductible to the business without the requirement to continue working. The plan's written provisions help define expectations for you and the employees buying the business. Some of the disadvantages include no access to company benefits and earnings are subject to ordinary income taxes and self-employment payroll taxes. The plans must be a written document drafted by an experienced attorney, ideally several years prior to your exit.

Salary continuation plans offer another potential advantage. Depending on accounting practices and tax status, the value of the contingent liability may need to be carried on the business' financial statements. Increasing liabilities without a corresponding increase in assets weakens financial statements and potentially lowers the business's value. Ironically this may be to your advantage.

Playbook: Lost Wages

Lost wages are payments to an employee to make up for a period of time when that employee received below market compensation. Many owners went through periods when they paid themselves low or even no wages. Comparing these periods against typical compensation for similar positions based on industry, business size and location generates a pool of "lost wages" that may be paid to you now or at exit.

The advantages of lost wages include: reasonable payments are income tax deductible to the business, no requirement to continue working and the specified amount of lost wages helps manage everybody's expectations. Some of the disadvantages include no access to company benefits, earnings are subject to ordinary income taxes and your advisors will need to prepare a compensation study to calculate and validate the lost wages amounts.

Playbook: Asset Lease Backs

One of the tactics to reduce your Exit Magic Number is to purchase assets used by the business, such as commercial real estate, and lease them back to the business. Asset lease backs also help sell to your employees. While the assets leased back to the business may be included in the sale, consider holding them and continuing the lease with the new owners. Supplement the business sale agreement with a long term lease at the highest reasonable rates. Lease payments are usually tax deductible to the business. Lease income is subject to ordinary income taxes, but typically not payroll taxes.

Playbook: Employee Stock Ownership Plan (ESOP)

Imagine the opportunity to sell the business and pay no income taxes. Imagine the flexibility to sell pieces of the business over time at your discretion to control the timing and terms of exit. Imagine employees financially motivated to increase the business's value along the way. If it sounds too good to be true, it may not be. It is an ESOP.

Employee Stock Ownership Plans (ESOPs) are perhaps the most powerful and least understood exit tool available to Innies. First created in the 1970s, the central idea behind ESOPs is that businesses grow faster and more profitably if all employees enjoy the financial rewards of ownership. There are about 10,000 ESOPs today, the vast majority at closely-held businesses.[*]

ESOPs are a type of retirement plan that has two special capabilities. First, ESOPs may invest primarily in the sponsoring business's stock. ESOPs are excluded from prudent investor rules that mandate diversified investment offerings inside a retirement plan. Second, an ESOP may borrow money. Combine these and you have a ready-made buyer for your business stock with cash. ESOPs have many uses, such as motivating employees toward business growth or raising capital on a tax favorable basis. Our concern is the potential role in your exit planning.

Perhaps the most attractive exit planning feature of ESOPs is the opportunity to defer or permanently avoid taxes on any gain resulting from the sale. (That's one of the few places in this book you will read

---

[*] The National Center for Employee Ownership, 2007.

"permanently avoid taxation".) Selling your business stock to an ESOP avoids triggering capital gains taxes if several conditions are met, including:

- The ESOP must be established as a C corporation. Owners of S corporations are not eligible for the tax deferral upon sale. (For this reason, it may be prudent to consider converting to a C corporation prior to establishing an ESOP in an S corporation.)

- You must have owned the stock for at least three years.

- The ESOP must own at least 30% of the company stock after the sale.

- You must reinvest the sale proceeds in what is known as Qualified Replacement Property (QRP) within a specified time frame. QRP includes common or preferred stock, bonds, and debt instruments issued by US domestic corporations that use more than 50% of their assets in an active trade or business.

The QRP generates potential income for financial freedom, particularly through dividend paying stocks and corporate bonds. As long as you stay invested in QRP, taxes from the business sale are deferred. If you invest in ineligible vehicles at some point in the future, then taxes would be due. Under current tax laws if the QRP is held until death, taxes that were never triggered are eliminated.* Thus you sold the business and never paid any taxes on the sale.

With the potential to sell for no income taxes, Innies considering an ESOP want the business be valued as highly as possible; tactics that reduce the business's value as discussed earlier do not apply. It's a powerful example of the need for the exit plan to dictate the business valuation results. A formal business appraisal is required to establish and maintain an ESOP.

Like with other qualified retirement plans, all eligible employees must be included in the ESOP. What if you want to sell the business to a specific employee or set of employees? There are several ways to accomplish this. Employees with higher wages usually receive a larger amount of business stock through the ESOP, much the same way they would receive more cash in a traditional retirement plan. If the employees who intend to buy your business are your highest paid, they will have the most ownership through the ESOP. Another approach involves selling only part of the business to the

---

*At death, assets with unrealized taxable gains step in value (basis) to the fair market value. This "step up in basis" wipes out any capital gains taxes. Congress is not doing this to be nice. The QRP assets you own at death are still subject to potential estate taxes.

ESOP (minimum of 30%) and the remainder directly to the top employees. The amount sold directly to employees will be taxable, but it may be a solution to secure some tax benefits and pass control of the business to your hand picked team.

Despite their advantages, ESOPs are clearly not for all businesses. Subchapter S corporations do not qualify for the tax deferred rollover treatment. Partnerships and most professional corporations are prohibited from installing ESOPs. These plans are complex and expensive. Costs to establish an ESOP can be tens or hundreds of thousands of dollars. Ongoing business valuation and other fees will be incurred. When employees participating in the ESOP retire or die, their shares must be repurchased. Consult with your advisors far ahead of your desired exit age. You may need to make considerable changes to your business to take full advantage of this tool.

Issue Three: Reducing Default Risk

Employees usually have little cash and little ability to raise cash on their own. Innies have to help their employees buy the business, either by taking paper at sale (commonly called owner financing or installment sale), pledging the business as collateral against a loan or both.* The risks for you are clear. If the business falters after your exit, the employees (who have become the owners) may be unable pay you. If the business fails your entire financial freedom and business legacy may be lost.

Returned to Seller

Jeremy owned a large long-distance trucking company. He founded the business nearly twenty years earlier. Jeremy was only 53 when we met him for the first time, but he looked at least ten years older. "I'm tired," he shared during our first meeting, and he looked it.

Jeremy had sold his business three years earlier to his long-time minority owner Dale. Dale had tried his best to carry on the business, but Dale either was not prepared or not capable.

---

* Before agreeing to an installment sale with your key employee/buyer, discuss the issue with your tax and other advisors. Installment sales are governed by a series of regulations that can provide tax benefits or nasty surprises depending on your situation.

Dale fell so far behind in the payments that he was forced to return the business to Jeremy. Now Jeremy was rebuilding just to get the business back in the black, and he had no idea how he long it would be before he could try to exit again.

Good news is many of the tactics already introduced reduce default risk. A low or zero Exit Magic Number reduces your financial dependency on the business, which increases flexibility to balance your wishes against the business's capacity. For example, if you want to sell to your employees for $10 million but have relatively little wealth outside the business, you probably need to get paid a large amount up front. This strains business's cash flow, potentially to the breaking point. With some wealth outside the business prior to exit, you may consider options that accommodate the business' financial resources. Reducing taxes can reduce default risk because fewer dollars are sent to the government. An orderly transfer of control potentially smoothes transitions and increases everyone's confidence of success. The following plays for the Playbook may further reduce default risk:

Playbook: Transfer the Risk

One solution to reduce or eliminate your vulnerability to default risk is to transfer the risk to a third party. Under this tactic, the employees who are buying the business purchase an annuity from an insurance company. The annuity will make installment payments to you rather than payments coming from the business. Commonly the insurance company guarantees the payments according to the terms of the annuity contract, eliminating your default risk. The employees receive a discount because purchasing a future income stream costs less than paying the full value upfront. For example, assume the payments are $500,000 per year for five years totaling $2.5 million. Your buyers may be able to purchase the annuity for 10-25% less than $2.5 million due to the time value of money discount. To further spread out your risk, use several different insurance companies each with high credit worthiness ratings.

Consider a similar tactic using zero coupon US government bonds for any balloon payments in your transaction. Rather than holding the balloon and the risk, have the employees buying the business purchase for you US

Treasury bonds called zero coupon bonds, or strips.* When the bond matures, you receive the cash. Bonds from the US government are considered risk free. (If the US federal government defaults on its payments, all of us likely have far bigger problems on our hands.) Like with an annuity, the buyer gets a significant discount on the price of the bond versus its face value. One downside is "zero coupon" bonds do not make interest payments during the time leading up to the maturity date but you, as the bond holder, incur income taxes each year on the accrued interest. It may be a small price to pay for potential peace of mind.

Playbook: Insurance on the Employees/Buyers

As long as you are at financial risk, require the employees who will purchase the business to maintain adequate life and disability insurance sufficient to pay the remaining balance should something happen. Your bank or other lender probably has made the same requirement of you at some point. Consider the same requirement for your buyers for the same reasons.

Playbook: Golden Handcuffs Plans

One of the tactics to reduce risk of a key employee defecting before your exit was Golden Handcuffs plans. (See Chapter Three.) These plans create a future cash reward large enough to motivate the key employee to stay, regardless what other temptations might come along. This same play can serve a second purpose for Innies. If you implement Golden Handcuffs plans for key employees and create a fund for the future benefits (you are not obligated to fund the future benefits but may pay them out of business cash flows), the employees may apply those dollars once vested toward the business purchase. This "supercharges" the plan: you reduce risk of top employees leaving now and the employees are accumulating cash which reduces default risk.

---

* The term "zero coupon" comes from the days when bonds had coupons, usually along the bottom, that needed to be clipped off and turned in to receive the periodic interest payment. A bond that did not pay interest had no coupons.

I'll Take Every Percent I Can Get

Hank knew two things about the top three employees in his distribution business: he did not want to risk losing them and one day he expected to sell the business to them. The questions Hank had struggled with were how to keep them until his exit, and how to reduce the amount of owner financing Hank would have to provide.

To answer both issues, Hank implemented a golden handcuffs plan. The plan was funded with key person life insurance on all three employees. The death benefit protected the business should any employee die prior to Hank's exit, while the policies' cash values provided the funding for future cash rewards. At Hank's exit, the employees expected to apply the cash toward the business purchase.

Based on the projected cash value increase, it appeared the golden handcuffs plan could grow to nearly 10% of the estimated future business price. Upon seeing this, Hank responded, "Well, they've got nothing now. I'll take every percent I can get. The way I look at it, that's 10% less than I have to worry about plus they won't leave between now and then."

Conclusion

Successfully selling to valued, trusted employees can be a crowning accomplishment in your time as a business owner. You potentially create a business legacy, provide an opportunity for your employees and achieve personal financial freedom in the process. With help from advisors, follow these steps to move downfield toward a future dance in the end zone:

1) Answer the Seven Essential Questions (Chapter Two)

2) Take prudent risk management steps (Chapter Three)

3) Reduce your Exit Magic Number (Chapter Four)

4) Set your game plan for meeting the issues most Innies face (this Chapter)

Key Points for Innies:

• If you have little confidence in your employees' ability to lead the business then everything else is moot.

• Start immediately filling any holes in your management team.

• The combined tax bill between you and the employees who purchase the business can easily reach 69% of the business's price.

• In many cases, Innies benefit by reducing the potential value of the business and replacing it with compensation-based programs to help achieve financial freedom.

• If the business falters after your exit, the employees (who have become the owners) may be unable pay you. Reducing default risk is a critical challenge for Innies.

Proceed to the last two chapters (starting on page 174) to address life after exit and finish your game plan for dancing in the end zone.

8

The Squeezer's Game Plan

Your business may be highly successful. It may be a market leader, employ many people, generate large annual revenues or produce substantial profits. Despite these achievements, Squeezers recognize that nobody is likely to pay for their business's goodwill (its value as a going concern). Squeezers are common. Many professional service businesses are inextricably tied to the talents or relationships of the owner. Many industries offer little to no barrier of entry, making it easy for competition to get started or build market share without writing a check for your business. Squeezers are not limited to small closely-held businesses. We work with the owners of a construction company with more than $100 million annual revenues who believe, probably correctly, that nobody will buy their business beyond a couple million dollars for equipment. They know their path to financial freedom requires squeezing the business dry along the way.

Two great misconceptions exist about Squeezers. The first is Squeezers do not need exit planning. When outlining this book, a number of people said to me something like, "Well, you won't need a chapter for Squeezers. They have nothing to do." Admittedly Squeezers have it simpler in many ways. You do not need to navigate the tax, financial, legal and other issues of passing the business to family, selling to outsiders or transitioning to top employees. But simple does not mean the same as easy. Among the four exit strategies, Squeezers alone face the near certainty that there is no pot of gold at the end of the rainbow. Passers can receive income from the business after exit, and Innies and Outies can convert at exit future equity to achieve financial freedom. Aside from selling business assets at exit, Squeezers are entirely dependent on current cash for personal financial freedom. In many ways, poor exit planning endangers the Squeezer more than any other owner. This chapter is shorter than others, but Squeezers' margin for error is thinner.

The second misconception is closing a business is a sign of failure. The conventional wisdom's emphasizing on business succession would have you believe this. If the business survives, that is success; if the business does not continue, that is failure. A planned liquidation at exit is quite different from closing down due to mismanagement or calamity. Planned liquidation is the natural outcome of millions of successful closely-held businesses. Being a Squeezer is not a sign of failure but rather the conclusion of a successful career and business venture.

The first four chapters provided an exit planning foundation for all business owners. Squeezers must get the foundational work correct. For example, you must thoroughly address risk management because everything rests on you. (See Chapter Three.) From here, we focus on the Squeezer's game plan. Most Squeezers face three issues unique to their exit strategy:

1) Reduce Exit Magic Number to Zero

2) Orderly Transition for Employees and Customers

3) Orderly Liquidation of the Business

Issue One: Reduce Exit Magic Number to Zero

All owners benefit from efforts to lower their Exit Magic Number because it increases flexibility to favorably align the Three Ts: timing, terms and taxes. Squeezers must go one step further. Aside from the value of any assets you could sell at exit, your Exit Magic Number must be zero or you cannot reach financial freedom. The Exit Magic Number reflects your financial dependency on your business. A higher number means you are more dependent on the business, specifically its earnings. If your Exit Magic Number is greater than zero, it simply means you cannot afford to exit from your business given your lifestyle and income expectations.

Squeezers cannot expect a "liquidity event" at exit, other than selling off any assets the business may possess. You must rely on current-cash based methods to convert your business's value into financial freedom. In many ways your situation is the same as the tens of millions of working Americans who do not own closely-held businesses. Like them, you must start now putting away money for your retirement or other post exit goals. Unlike them you face a greater tax burden and must balance the business's needs with your own. The systematic tools discussed in Chapter Four to convert current cash into wealth outside the business are the essential plays for your playbook. Carefully review these tools and implement those which tax efficiently reduce your Exit Magic Number to zero by your target exit age.

Issue Two: Orderly Transition for Employees and Customers

Regardless of their exit strategy, many owners feel a strong need to fairly treat valued employees, customers and other close relationships at exit. Financial freedom at the cost of out of work employees or stranded customers might not be acceptable. Squeezers face an additional challenge with employees and customers. Well before your exit, employees and customers might conclude your business cannot meet their long term needs. It's not difficult for them to reach this conclusion. If you are significantly older than some employees, or if customers desire a business relationship that lasts beyond your normal retirement age, they may grow concerned. Employees who are younger than you want to avoid losing their jobs when you exit. Customers may be sensitive to the business's ability to service them down the road. Squeezers cannot afford employees or customers leaving now because of a future exit.

Too Young and Too Old

Will was a highly successful OB-GYN with his own medical clinic. He was healthy, active and 58 when we first met. Will shared that he would prefer to work until age 65 or 70, but doubted it would happen. When we asked why, he replied, "Because it's harder and harder for me to get new patients each year. Most new patients are going to be younger women. Some of them prefer a female doctor, but nearly all of them prefer a doctor who is not twenty or thirty years older. I can't blame them if they don't want to have to change doctors down the road."

Will did not want to exit before he was ready because of a declining customer base. We spoke further and he added, "I know the easy solution is to bring in a younger doctor, but I don't want to hire and train a new colleague or partner at this point. I'd give up much of my freedom. I'm too young to retire and too old for new patients."

At some point your future exit becomes obvious, and people important to the business wonder how it impacts them. Do not ignore the issue. Identify steps to assure employees, customers and prospects that they will not suffer if you exit before their needs are met.

Negotiate well in advance of your exit age a new service provider to assume or purchase your customer relationships. Be open with people. They may be thinking about this already and can worry without guidance from you. Your top employees probably do not want to leave you—they want to avoid getting surprised or having too little time to find new careers. Communicate early a genuine willingness to help them transit to quality new opportunities when your exit date arrives. Golden Handcuffs plans with a "stay bonus" tied to your target exit age can be extremely effective. (See Chapter Four.)

Issue Three: Orderly Liquidation of the Business

Hopefully you have quite a few good years left in you and your business before exit. Time helps with preparation, especially with complex and unfamiliar situations such as closing a business. Shutting down creates legal considerations, triggers various potential taxes and presents management challenges. While much of the actual work happens toward the end, preparation helps minimize mistakes and missed opportunities.

Playbook: Business Wrap Up Plan

Discuss with your advisors the likely steps involved to wrap up your business in an orderly manner. Identify any steps that need implemented today. Cover the following:

- Discuss the legal procedures to properly shut down the business. Lay out any steps to reduce risk of creditors or claims against the business after your exit.

- If you have assets to sell at exit, identify tax implications and steps that could reduce taxes. For example, selling appreciated assets from a C corporation creates the potential for double-taxation at your exit.

- List the proper steps to terminate contracts such as equipment leases, employment agreements and customer agreements. Pay special attention to provisions and requirements that may extend beyond your target exit age. For example, verify that real estate and equipment leases do not continue past your intended exit age.

- Discuss the steps required to terminate the retirement plan and other employee benefit plans. Some benefits programs require careful planning or you risk incurring costs after exit.

- Identify the local, state and federal agencies to notify. Forgetting a business license or permit renewal may increase unnecessary costs.

Conclusion

Squeezers usually do not create a lasting business legacy, but the personal legacy may be an important part of your vision for exit success. Your business has favorably touched the lives of customers, employees, family and others. Celebrate with these people achievements up to and including the exit. With help from advisors, follow these steps to move downfield toward a future dance in the end zone:

1) Answer the Seven Essential Questions (Chapter Two)

2) Take prudent risk management steps (Chapter Three)

3) Reduce your Exit Magic Number to zero (Chapter Four)

4) Set your game plan for addressing issues many Squeezers face (this Chapter)

Key Points for Squeezers:

- In many ways inadequate exit planning endangers Squeezers more than other owners.

- Squeezers must use the business's current cash flow and not future equity to achieve financial freedom; your Exit Magic Number usually must be zero by the target exit age.

- Address how employees and customers will have their needs met after your exit.

- Identify steps that need to be taken now to facilitate closing the business at your exit.

Proceed to the last two chapters (starting on page 174) to address life after exit and finish your game plan for dancing in the end zone.

9

Life After Exit

Owners fall into three groups: those who can't wait to exit, those who hope it never happens and some who waver between the two. Many owners love their business life and have little interest in anything else. Your sense of self-worth is rooted in your identity as a business leader, creator and achiever. If you were not passionate about your business, almost certainly it would not have survived and prospered. Why think about something you don't want to do much less plan for it to happen?

Planning for a life after exit is important regardless of how you feel today about this topic. As discussed several times in this book, you are not in complete control of your exit timing. An accident or illness could take you away from the business today. A surprise buyer may walk through your door today. I have witnessed owners on the verge of selling get cold feet because they had no idea what they would do after the sale. With more time they might have been able to figure it out before the potential buyer took its cash elsewhere.

If pursuing a life after exit is not exciting today, your mind might change sooner than you expect. We discussed in Chapter One that some owners put off exit planning because of "irrational entrepreneurialism"—a passionate optimism that sustains owner's enthusiasm for the business deep into working years. A byproduct of irrational entrepreneurialism is owners' feelings toward life after exit can change quickly. Rather than gradually warm to life after exit like many working Americans who gradually welcome retirement, business owners often remain steadfast against life after exit until one day waking up and feeling it couldn't happen soon enough. When the entrepreneurialism starts to wear off, it can go rather quickly. Time reduces the number of owners who never want a life after exit.

Like other components of exit planning, waiting to think about this topic risks undermining your end zone dance. Financial wealth cannot fill the void of life without meaningful challenges and purpose. Peace of mind shares equal importance with financial freedom in the definition of exit success.

It's a Better Hobby than Job

Other than raise his family, Leon had done only two things his entire adult life: build a highly successful manufacturing business and work on his farm. He loved both activities, frequently working at the manufacturing plant Monday through Friday and farming at least one full day each weekend. After nearly thirty years in business, he was approached by a private equity group with a $29 million offer to purchase his manufacturing business. Leon convened his exit planning team to discuss the offer. We agreed the price was attractive. Warren, Leon's attorney for twenty years, asked his client, "Leon, what are you going to do with yourself if you sell?"

"Farm full time," was Leon's quick reply. He spent twenty minutes telling us how much he's always loved the farm. If he sold the manufacturing business he could farm all week long and never have a financial worry. Warren pushed Leon a little harder on the issue, but Leon said he was excited by the opportunity. Leon took the offer.

For months Leon was happy. Then something happened. About eight months after selling Leon called and asked us if we could help him find another business to buy. Surprised, I asked what had happened.

He said, "Now I know why for all those years I worked in the plant five days a week and farmed one day a week. I love farming—but one day a week not five. It's a better hobby than job. I can't do this for the next twenty years of my life."

Whether life after exit is recreational or you pursue other business ventures, it is important to identify activities that give stimulation and mental rewards like those your business provided. The following tactics for your Playbook may help prepare for a fulfilling life after exit:

Playbook: Reallocate Time and Talents

Even if you continue working as a consultant or employee after exit, at some point your available time will increase. This could be scary or a moment to relish. If unclear about what you will do, meet with loved ones and advisors to brainstorm on how to reallocate your time and talents. Have fun with the process. Be creative. (Haven't you ever said, "I wish I had more time for that…"?) Consider the following questions for help:

- *What does your Ideal Schedule look like?* What would you like to do each day, week or month? Open a calendar and write out the Ideal Schedule. Be as specific as possible.

- *What are your greatest talents?* Undoubtedly some of your skills and talents are greater than others and contributed to your business successes. List them. The list probably represents not only what you are good at but also what you like to do.

- *Outside of your business, where can you apply your talents?* Who or what organizations, groups, causes, institutions could use you? Make a list of business, social, charitable or civic organizations you know or have been involved with on any level. Read your local newspapers for thirty days to identify businesses, groups, travel destinations, charities that could interest you. Investigate those that seem interesting or a potential fit.

Share your findings with close family and advisors. Ask for candid feedback. They may have perspective because they are on the outside looking in. You do not have to know all the answers today, and can change your mind anywhere along the way. Getting some initial ideas is a large step forward.

Playbook: Externships

Has your business ever hired interns? They usually work for little to no pay because they want experience working inside your business. Give yourself the same opportunity to gain experience *external* from your business with an Externship. Leon from the previous Real World Story deserves credit for this tactic. At the end of that memorable phone call he said to me, "I knew right away farming on a full time basis was not for me. I should have taken a few weeks off work before I sold my company just to try it. I wouldn't be stuck now."

Externships are opportunities to try a new career, activity or hobby. You don't have to tell anybody else you are on an "externship" if you are worried somebody will ask you to get coffee. The point simply is to try your ideas and see if you like them.

From Boardroom to Classroom

For years Wilson thought he could enjoy teaching after his children took over the business. He loved finance and believed his hard won experience as a successful owner would benefit future business leaders. Wilson never shared with anybody his thoughts until an exit planning meeting with his advisors and spouse Holly. "Sweetie," she said to him, "you'd be great." Still a little unsure, he agreed to try.

Wilson learned that a local college with an adult MBA program invited business leaders to guest lecture. He contacted the school and was readily accepted. One successful lecture became several, followed by a seat on an advisory board to the school. The more he got involved, the more he knew after exiting he wanted to teach finance to business students. Wilson later shared with me that giving up control of his business to his children was his greatest fear in his exit planning, but the issue became easier to handle knowing he had another passion to pursue.

Externships can be formal (serving on the school advisory board) or informal (farming for two straight weeks). The goal is to gain experience. If you have always wanted to make furniture, take a vacation, not to play golf or travel, but to take a woodworking class and make furniture. Live your Ideal Schedule for a week, month or longer. (If your business cannot afford for you to take that much time away, it illustrates the need for more management development as part of your exit planning.) Try out different activities while you are still an owner because there's no pressure to make a decision or time vacuum to fill. Internships work for college kids because they gain experience before they need a job. Externships work for business owners because you can gain experience and insight before you enter life after exit.

Conclusion

The thought of exiting your business may be stressful and unwelcome. Part of what causes discomfort is the lack of guidelines—this may be one of the few moments in life when you can do almost anything. Avoid finding yourself without the sense of purpose and value that contributes to peace of mind. Turn the uncertainty into an opportunity. Be creative and have fun. These tactics help bridge your world today as an owner with a future life after exit.

Key Points:

- **Planning for a life after exit is important. If do not look forward to doing something else, you may change your mind or exit from the business sooner than anticipated.**

- **Whether life after exit is recreational or involves new business ventures, identify activities that challenge and stimulate you using the talents and skills you've developed as a business owner.**

- **Investigate opportunities using "externships" between now and your inevitable exit.**

10

Your Next Play (Where to Go From Here)

There's a trick to the graceful exit. It begins with the vision to recognize when a job, a life stage, a relationship is over—and to let it go. It means leaving what's over without denying its value.

Ellen Goodman

Growing and leading your business up to this point probably has been one of your life's greatest accomplishments. While performance can bring personal wealth, for many it is not just about money. Deep satisfaction comes from building something from nothing (or from very little), creating jobs, delivering quality products or services and providing for loved ones. Your achievement is that much greater knowing your business has succeeded while so many others do not. If building and growing a closely-held business was easy more people would do it.

In the beginning, many owners do not cherish working on their exit. Some view exiting as the end of a journey they would prefer not finish. If you are happy and successful, why bother with exit planning at all? Nobody wants to exit from a happy marriage or rewarding friendship. One of this book's goals is to change owners' perspective about exit. A successful exit is the capstone on your business successes. It's the opportunity to control your finances, lifestyle and legacy. Isn't that at least part of the reason why you decided to own your own business in the first place—to be in control of your own future? Where do you go from here? Pull out your Playbook and get started.

Step One: Draft Your Team

The Core Team

An effective plan must consider tax, legal and financial issues. Proper strategy and tactics in these three areas drive exit success; poor planning in these areas can weaken or outright block efforts to get to the end zone. You must have an accountant, lawyer and financial advisor with direct experience helping business owners exit. These advisors join you and your closest family members form the Core Team. Consider the Core Team to be your starting offensive and defensive players.

The term "advisor" here is not just a catch-all word for the people or firms that you have done business with in the past. "Advisor" should mean a person or firm whose advice you seek *before* making an important decision. For example, the accountant you see only once per year during income tax season might not be a close advisor. The same standard applies to legal, financial and other professionals with whom you have worked up to this point. This is to not suggest the professionals you currently use are incapable of serving as exit advisors—if you are not seeking their advice before making important decisions perhaps you are not asking.

Ideally your current accountants, lawyers and financial advisors possess the relevant skills and experience. If you are unsure, verify if current advisors can provide the required assistance. Do not put loyalty in front of quality advice. Meet individually with your current advisors, explain what you want to accomplish and ask if they can help. In my experience, most professionals will honestly answer if they or their firms can meet your needs. If necessary, ask them to share examples and references from three clients whom they guided through this process. Ideally they provide examples similar to your current situation.

If current relationships do not have the required experience, select a new advisor in that profession with relevant expertise. Do not be somebody's guinea pig. This does not mean you must end the existing relationship. You may decide to continue working with that professional if his knowledge and experience with you and your business brings value. Perhaps your trusted general corporate attorney may not be qualified to meet all your exit planning legal needs but has worked for you for many years. Ask this attorney to join the Core Team but also recommend another lawyer or firm which has the missing expertise. It may not be ideal to have and pay two lawyers (or accountants, etc.) for one job, but you need advisors who know *both* exit planning and your business. It may be hard to get both from one source.

If you are filling open positions on the Core Team from scratch, ask trusted friends or business colleagues for referrals. Make interviewing and selecting the new advisor a priority in your busy schedule. Discuss the following items in your meetings to determine a good fit with your needs:

- Ask candidates to share at least three relevant stories of how they have helped other successful owners exit from their closely-held businesses.

- Request references. Follow up on the references or have an advisor already installed on the Core Team do this for you.

- Review how this individual or organization is compensated. Ask for written verification.

- Share your known answers to the Seven Essential End Zone Questions and ask the candidate to explain how he can assist in achieving your exit goals.

Your tax, legal and financial advisors plus close family members represent most owners' Core Team. Add any additional people who offer trusted, relevant advice but don't let the Core Team grow too large to be unwieldy. More than five or six individuals can become cumbersome.

The Support Team

Your specific exit strategy and the amount of time before your ideal exit age dictate if the Core Team needs additional help. The Support Team consists of professionals who facilitate a specific transaction or address a narrow issue. They are the special teams players in our football analogy; they only come on the field in specific circumstances. For example, Passers may need a business valuation expert to appraise the business to facilitate transferring ownership to a child or other heir. Outies usually need an intermediary (business broker, mergers and acquisition consultant, investment banker, etc.) to sell the business once exit is near. Rely on your Core Team to identify if and when to bring in that help and to recommend quality people or firms in the needed area.

Step Two: Openly Designate a Quarterback

Within your Core Team openly designate a quarterback. The football analogy works too well here to ignore it. You are the head coach. You set the objectives and decide who gets on the playing field. The quarterback's role is to lead your team down the field in an effective and timely manner toward the end zone. Too many owners get in trouble because they miss this step, or intentionally skip it because they fear ego conflict among the Core Team. Failing to have a clearly designated quarterback leaves your team either without a leader or with too many leaders. Neither works well.

Selecting a quarterback is essential. You may not have the time and almost certainly do not have the experience to coordinate each team member's activities. Like with a football team, your quarterback is expected to lead but not win the game on his own. The quarterback has no more authority than any other team member, and should not prevent any other team member from communicating with you. (This is often what leads to ego battles.) The quarterback has three distinct responsibilities:

1) Drive the process: schedule meetings, manage deadlines and meet time-sensitive goals.

2) Coordinate communications between the Core Team when you are not directly involved (run the huddle on the field).

3) Produce and keep current a written game plan that the entire Core Teams supports.

Any member of the Core Team can be the quarterback. Ideally the quarterback should be the advisor with the broadest experience so he can see your big picture. The quarterback also must have sufficient time to focus on your needs now and in the future. When you have determined the quarterback, clearly communicate this to the Core Team.

Step Three: Huddle Your Team

Once you have drafted your Core Team and selected the quarterback, convene a meeting as soon as possible. At the first meeting with your Core Team consider the following:

- Introduce team members who do not know one another.

- Define your exit planning objectives and emphasize you want to grow your business in a manner that achieves your objectives.

- Discuss the Seven Essential End Zone Questions, share the answers you have and identify how unanswered questions will be addressed.

Also during the first Core Team meeting, review and discuss the following best practices to maximize effectiveness and results:

- Clearly define which team member has primary responsibility on any action item or issue. For example, if a new buy-sell plan is needed for your business then your attorney is responsible for the written agreement, your financial advisor must recommend insurance or other funding vehicles and your accountant needs to evaluate the ideal tax structure. The quarterback is accountable for *monitoring progress* on each item.

- Authorize and expect the Core Team to communicate directly with each other. The team needs to be able to share information and brainstorm about your needs when you are not in the room. This saves time (especially yours), allows them to cover highly technical issues and collaborate without worrying about "the client" watching. Failing to do this is like the football coaching telling the team to never huddle up and talk to each other on the field. It may be necessary in today's environment concerning confidentiality to sign a release form permitting the team to share information with each other. There is one important exception. While it's not common, you may encounter an issue that is sensitive enough to require the attorney-client protection. Ask your attorney to identify any issue that could require the need to meet alone to preserve this protection.

- The Core Team should strive for consensus before making recommendations. Consensus is achievable on most issues between knowledgeable advisors who put the client's needs first. However exit planning raises complex issues and many of the planning tactics and tools are complex instruments. In the event the team cannot agree upon an issue, do not play referee or try to evaluate a highly technical matter. Ask them to explain how and why they are not in agreement. Instruct differing team members to *list in writing* the pros and cons of the issue or matter. At that point you will need to weigh the issue and decide, or seek an outside opinion if necessary.

- Meet at a location away from your business such as one of the team member's offices. Rotate offices if this helps ego-management among the Core Team members. Protect your privacy from employees and customers. During meetings turn off cell phones and eliminate other distractions. Your exit planning should command full attention.

- Decide on a regular meeting schedule. At first, when you are creating your plan and have a healthy to-do list, consider meeting every few weeks. Once much of the initial work is complete, meet two to four times per year with the Core Team to monitor and update the plan. As exit draws near resume more frequent meetings if needed. The quarterback is responsible for keeping you and the Core Team on schedule.

Step Four: Put Together Your Written Game Plan

Your exit plans must be in writing. In most cases the quarterback should bear responsibility for producing a written document and keeping it up-to-date. All members of the Core Team should review and approve its contents. A written plan should:

- Define your exit objectives and priorities.

- Identify time frames and deadlines for completing tasks.

- Provide a tool to hold team members accountable for accurate and timely results.

- Provide a commonly accepted set of facts, assumptions and other data for the Core Team to reference in their work.

- Effectively brief Support Team members if and when they join the planning process.

- Track pending and completed action items to monitor progress and prevent anything from falling into cracks.

A written exit plan can take nearly any form or length, but to be effective the following best practices should be considered:

- The plan should use easy to understand, non-technical language; if technical language is necessary adequate definitions or a glossary should be provided.

- Any assumptions, such as the business' value, inflation rates, tax rates and investment results should be clearly disclosed.

- Important deadlines or due dates should be summarized and a method for tracking deadlines should be included.

- Family members and top employees should know how to access a copy of the exit plan in the event of an emergency. Contact information for the Core Team members should be included for the same purpose.

- The exit plan should reference how to locate important tax, legal, accounting or financial documents that are related to the plan, such as buy-sell agreements, financial statements, insurance policies, etc.

- The exit plan should be clearly labeled and dated so updates are easily distinguishable.

Step Five: Update the Game Plan as You Go

Watch a football game on television and a short time into the game the sports broadcasters will point out "adjustments" that one or both coaches make as the game progresses. These adjustments are changes in strategy and tactics one team makes in reaction to its movement—or lack of movement—down the field. Like the football coach, you must anticipate changes to your plan. The changes may be external: tax reform, market conditions, interest rates or industry trends. The changes may be internal: business results, family status or personal health to name a few. A sound exit plan must be flexible. Owners must expect change to occur and team members must stay engaged throughout the process. Here-today-gone-tomorrow advisors do little good.

The quarterback should convene the Core Team and owner at least twice per year to review and monitor the plan. Schedule at least one meeting about 45-60 days before the business's fiscal year end to allow time for actions that may be sensitive to fiscal or tax deadlines. Written updates to the plan should be circulated among the Core Team, any Support Team members and family as needed.

Conclusion

Exit is inevitable. Even if you prefer to work until your health or life are exhausted, you must address how your exit impacts family, employees, customers and the business legacy. Your future deserves your present attention; undoubtedly you have worked too hard and accomplished too much to surrender control over the eventual outcome. Failing to plan ahead risks denying yourself and others the chance to dance in the end zone.

There may be moments during this journey that are not enjoyable. While the proven strategies and tactics in this book will help, you may face difficult issues. Your business, employees and customers, family, money and taxes are complex enough topics by themselves—exit planning must balance all of these areas and more. You may find yourself on uncertain ground without much personal experience to guide you; this may be your first and only exit from a closely-held business.

During these times, remember the good you are trying to accomplish. Planning tomorrow's exit helps create a better business today and benefits you and so many others tomorrow. In the first chapter we defined exit planning as *the conscious effort to efficiently grow and convert private business ownership into personal wealth to achieve financial freedom and peace of mind*. Exit planning is about how you create value in your business and how you convert that value to achieve your personal and business goals. Said slightly differently, exit planning is taking a few extra steps while on a long and sometimes challenging journey to assure that the rewards you achieve, the lessons you learn and the opportunities you create are shared with as many people as possible for as long as possible.

Appendices

Appendix 1. Exit Planning Playbook

The tactics and tools presented in *Dance in the End Zone* constitute your Exit Planning Playbook. Just as the football coach selects plays that give his team the best chance to reach the end zone, you and your advisors can select the plays that best fit your exit planning needs. The following alphabetical list summarizes the primary purpose and identifies where the play is discussed in the book.

NAME OF PLAY	PRIMARY PURPOSE	CHAPTER(S)
Adopt a M.O.O.S.E.	Lower Exit Magic Number	4
Asset Lease Backs	Lower Exit Magic Number	4,5,7
Business Growth Plan	Build transferable value	6
Business Wrap Up Plan	Orderly close of business operations	8
Buy-Sell Plans	Avoid unwanted co-owners	3
Charitable Remainder Trust	Favorably align the timing, terms and taxes of exit	6
Compare Your Seven Essential Questions	Address co-owners with opposing exit agendas	3
Consulting Company	Favorably align the timing, terms and taxes of exit	5,6,7
Control Checkpoints	Transfer control in orderly manner	5,7
Convert C to an S Corporation	Favorably align the timing, terms and taxes of exit	6
Create Multiple Exit Plans	Address co-owners with opposing exit agendas	3
Desirable Contracts	Build transferable value	6

NAME OF PLAY	PRIMARY PURPOSE	CHAPTER(S)
Devalue the Business then Give It Away	Transfer ownership in an orderly manner	5
Diversified Customer Base	Build transferable value	6
Document How Your Business Works	Build transferable value	6
Emergency Guidance Letter	Address risk of losing you	3
Employee Stock Ownership Plan (ESOP)	Favorably align the timing, terms and taxes of exit	7
Employment Agreement	Protect against loss of key employee	3
Employment Contracts	Favorably align the timing, terms and taxes of exit	5,6,7
Externships	Plan for life after exit	9
Family Balancer Trust	Treat all heirs fairly	5
Family Business Council	Transfer control in orderly manner	5
Family Development Budget	Transfer control in orderly manner	5
Golden Handcuffs Plans	Protect against loss of key employee	3, 7
Grantor Retained Annuity Trust	Transfer ownership in an orderly manner	5
Ideal "Strategic" Asset Allocation	Lower Exit Magic Number	4
Ideal Legal Business Entities	Favorably align the timing, terms and taxes of exit	6
Insurance on the Employees/Buyers	Reduce default risk	7
Intellectual Property	Build transferable value	6
Intentionally Defective Grantor Trust	Transfer ownership in an orderly manner	5
Irrevocable Life Insurance Trust	Providing adequate estate liquidity	5
Key Employee Life Insurance	Protect against loss of key employee	3
Lost Wages	Favorably align the timing, terms and taxes of exit	5,7
Maintain Adequate Insurance	Address risk of losing you	3
NewCo	Favorably align the timing, terms and taxes of exit	6

NAME OF PLAY	PRIMARY PURPOSE	CHAPTER(S)
Non-Voting Stock for Inactive Children	Treat all heirs fairly	5
Normalized Earnings	Build transferable value	6
One-Way Buy-Sell Plan	Transfer control in orderly manner	3,7
Parallel Business	Transfer ownership in an orderly manner	5
Personal Goodwill	Favorably align the timing, terms and taxes of exit	6
Powers of Attorney	Address risk of losing you	3
Readable and Reliable Financial Statements	Build transferable value	6
Reallocate Time and Talents	Plan for life after exit	9
Reinvest/Receive Ratio	Lower Exit Magic Number	4
Roth 401(k) Plans	Lower Exit Magic Number	4
Royalties and Earnouts	Favorably align the timing, terms and taxes of exit	6
Salary Continuation Plan	Favorably align the timing, terms and taxes of exit	5,7
Sale to Employees Feasibility Study	Transfer control in orderly manner	7
Section 1202	Favorably align the timing, terms and taxes of exit	6
Sell the Business for Minimum Reasonable Value	Favorably align the timing, terms and taxes of exit	7
Stock Swap	Favorably align the timing, terms and taxes of exit	6
Tax Analysis and Plan	Favorably align the timing, terms and taxes of exit	6
Tax Leveraged Retirement Plans	Lower Exit Magic Number	4
Transfer Default Risk	Reduce default risk	7
Upside Down Organizational Chart	Build transferable value	6

Appendix 2: White Horse Advisors 2008 Survey of Closely-Held Business Owners

White Horse Advisors is a leading firm in the area of exit planning services to owners of closely-held businesses and retirement plan sponsors. White Horse Advisors educates business owners about the advantages of succession planning and assist clients in developing solutions in areas such as exit strategies, estate planning, business continuity, retirement plans and investment strategies. White Horse Advisors sought to better understand the triggers that cause an owner to begin the exit planning process, as well as the decision process of selecting a succession planning advisor and exit planning services provider.

To that end, White Horse Advisors commissioned CMI to conduct the 2008 White Horse Advisors Survey of Closely-Held Business Owners. The research was conducted with a random selection of business owners across the country, pulled from membership of Vistage International. Vistage groups meet monthly, affording the opportunity to administer the paper surveys to the entire group of owners.

The survey was conducted between October 2007 and February 2008. A total of 58 groups participated in the study, representing 444 survey respondents. Significance testing is conducted at the 95% confidence level. At this confidence level, the data from 444 surveys has a precision level of +/- 4.65%.

For more information on this research and to download a copy of the research summary, visit www.exitplanningresearch.com.

Note

At various points this book references investment and insurance products. When properly designed and implemented, investment and insurance products can play an important role in achieving an owner's personal and business financial objectives.

It is important to note that investments will fluctuate and when redeemed may be worth more or less than originally invested. When considering the proper use of life insurance, note that insurance products contain fees, charges and may have additional limitations such as surrender charges. The primary reason to purchase a life insurance product is the death benefit. Regarding life insurance owned by your business, such as for key person coverage, the death benefit is income tax free to the business if the business, at the time of purchase, had met the requirements of Internal Revenue Code 101(j) including providing the insured with advance notice, obtaining the insured's prior consent to be insured and meeting insured's executive income requirements.

Tracking No. 33345/36531

DOFU 2008 12 5

For additional copies of this book, visit the
World Wide Association of Writers at
www.wwaow.com or the author's business
website at www.whitehorseadvisors.com.